The IMC Rating Question & Answer Simplifier

Philip Mathews & Jeremy M Pratt

The IMC Rating Question & Answer Simplifier
Philip Mathews & Jeremy M Pratt

ISBN 1-874783-51-9

First Edition 1996 published as:
The Questions and Answers Book for the IMC Rating

This Revised Edition 1999

Copyright © 1996 & 1999 CPM Enterprises Ltd & Airplan Flight Equipment Ltd

All rights reserved. No part of this publication may be reproduced, stored in a retrieval system, or transmitted in any form or by any means, electronic, mechanical, photocopy, recording, or otherwise, without the prior written permission of the copyright holder.

AFE

Published by:

Airplan Flight Equipment Ltd
1a Ringway Trading Estate, Shadowmoss Road, Manchester M22 5LH
Tel: 0161-499 0023   Fax: 0161-499 0298
www.airplan.u-net.com

Private Pilots Licence

THE EXAMINATION

CONDUCT OF THE EXAMINATION

The examination usually takes place at the Flying Training Organisation (FTO) under the supervision of a CAA authorised examiner.

Candidates are expected to provide their own navigation, writing & calculating equipment. Reference books, notes and electronic calculators are **not** permitted. The exam room will have any relevant posters or publications removed. The candidate would not normally be expected to leave and re-enter the exam room whilst the examination is in progress; so go to the toilet first!

The exam's specified time limit will be strictly observed. The person supervising the exam is not allowed to discuss the examination, interpretation of questions etc. whilst the examination is in progress. The exam question paper should not be marked in any way. Use the back of the answer sheet for any rough workings you want to do.

Once the exam is finished, the authorised examiner will mark the paper. In the event of a pass the examiner will discuss any questions wrongly answered. In the event of a fail, the examiner may indicate general areas of weakness, but will not discuss answers to specific questions.

There are three examination papers, it is not permitted to take the same paper twice. Should the candidate fail all three papers, arrangements will be made for an examination by a CAA staff examiner.

The candidate should be warned before the exam starts that any infringement of the rules will result in disqualification.

EXAMINATION TECHNIQUE

The examination is of multiple choice type – marks are **not** deducted for an incorrect answer.

Before starting the exam paper read through the instructions carefully. Check the time limit so that you know when the exam will finish.

Unless there are specific instructions otherwise, tackle the questions you are sure you can answer first, and return to difficult questions later. Read each question carefully and be sure you understand exactly what is being asked. There will be only one correct answer, sometimes you can reach this by eliminating the wrong answers.

You are not allowed spare paper, or to mark the examination paper in any way. Do any workings out on the back of the answer sheet.

The exam time limit can exert 'time-pressure'. All questions carry equal points so if time becomes a problem, work through questions that you are confident you can answer first, returning to more difficult questions afterwards. Remember that marks are not deducted for an incorrect answer, so if you really cannot select the correct answer for a question it is worth taking a guess.

Although good examination technique will help you make the best of your knowledge, it does not guarantee a pass. The best preparation for the exam is to learn the subject fully. Your FTO will not enter you for an exam unless they feel you know the subject well enough to have a good chance of passing. Even once you have passed an exam, you cannot assume that your knowledge of that subject is complete. You should regularly revise and update each subject to keep your knowledge current.

USE OF THIS PUBLICATION

To get the best out of this publication you should tackle each paper in order. After completing a paper mark your answers to assess your result. Review any questions you answered incorrectly to see if there is an area in which your knowledge is weak. If this is the case revise that area before attempting the next paper. The worked answers show how the answers have been arrived at, but a publictaion of this type cannot fully explore the full background to each subject area.

It must be stressed that you should review the whole of an area in which you are failing questions. This publication has been designed to test your complete knowledge of each subject area in the IMC syllabus. It is not possible to pass the exam by learning set answers to set questions.

Initially the time limit should be taken as a guide only. In later papers you should aim to be obtaining a pass mark within the specified time limit.

Remember the surest way to pass the exam is to know the subject thoroughly!

Questions and Answers for the IMC Rating **PAPER 1**

Instructions

1 Time allowed 2 hours.

2 Twenty five multi-choice questions each carrying 4 marks. Marks are not deducted for wrong answers. The pass mark is 72% (i.e. 18 questions or more must be answered correctly).

3 Unless otherwise specified, the questions relate to a UK licenced pilot, operating a UK registered aircraft in UK airspace.

4 Read each question carefully as there is only one answer which is correct.

5 Remember examination technique, you are advised to pass over questions that seem difficult at first sight and return to them when you have answered the others.

Questions and Answers
for the IMC Rating **PAPER 1**

1 A Private Pilot holding an IMC rating may not:

A Accept an IFR clearance in Class A airspace

B Fly out of sight of the surface

C Land when the flight visibility is 1800m

D Cross the base of an en-route section of an airway that is specified as a Flight Level when in VMC.

2 An IMC rating Certificate of Test is valid for a period of:

A 12 months

B 13 months

C 24 months

D 25 months.

3 You plan to fly IFR from A to B, outside controlled airspace. The highest obstacle within 5nm of track is 2400ft amsl. If your TRK (T) is 162° (variation 6° E) and the forecast pressure is 993mb, what is the lowest useable Quadrantal Level (assume 1mb = 30ft)?

A FL35

B FL55

C FL75

D FL95.

4 The forecast for your intended destination (which is outside controlled airspace) reads: 280900Z 281019 24012KT 3000 RA OVC012 BECMG 1517 1200 OVC008. Which of the following statements is correct?

A Conditions will remain within IMC rating limits throughout the period

B Conditions will be outside your landing limit throughout the period

C You should plan to arrive at your destination prior to 1500 hrs

D You should plan to arrive at your destination after 1500 hrs.

5 A pilot flying an approach in poor lighting conditions to a well-lit runway surrounded by featureless terrain, without glidepath guidance, is likely to:

A Fly an accurately judged approach

B Over estimate distance to the runway and consequently overshoot

C Have difficulty seeing the runway

D Think the runway is closer than it really is, and consequently fly too shallow an approach and undershoot.

Questions and Answers

PAPER 1 *for the I M C Rating*

Complete the attached flight plan using an ICAO 1:500,000 chart for Southern England, then answer questions 6-14.

6 What is the Magnetic track from BOVINGDON to COMPTON?

A 231°

B 235°

C 244°

D 249°.

7 What is the groundspeed for the leg between COMPTON and CHILBOLTON?

A 100kt

B 106kt

C 116kt

D 134kt.

8 Given that the QNH is 1013mb, what would be the lowest Quadrantal Cruising Level between COMPTON and CHILBOLTON?

A FL35

B FL40

C FL45

D FL50.

9 What is the total distance for the route from CLACTON to COMPTON ABBAS?

A 143.5nm

B 147nm

C 138.5nm

D 170nm.

10 What is the leg time between COMPTON ABBAS and YEOVIL?

A 3mins

B 6½mins

C 9½mins

D 15mins.

Questions and Answers
for the IMC Rating **PAPER 1**

11 If you set course overhead CLACTON at 1433 what will be your ETA at COMPTON ABBAS?

A 1543

B 1558

C 1603

D 1606.

12 What is the minimum fuel required for this flight (rounded up to the nearest litre):

Start, Taxy and Take-off	10lt
Clacton to Compton Abbas @ 30lt/hr	
Approach and Missed Approach	15lt
Alternate (Compton Abbas - Yeovil) @ 30lt/hr	
Holding 45mins @ 30lt/hr	
Approach and Landing	10lt
Reserve	30lt

A 101lt

B 109lt

C 115lt

D 128lt.

13 In addition to the London QNH, which regional pressure settings will be required for the flight from CLACTON to COMPTON ABBAS?

A Yarmouth, Chatham, Portland, Cotswold

B Yarmouth, Portland

C Cotswold, Portland

D Yarmouth, Chatham, Cotswold.

14 With regard to the leg between LAMBOURNE and BOVINGDON assume that Thames Radar will provide a Radar Information Service (RIS). Select the response that best describes the service:

A Traffic information will be passed and Thames Radar will provide avoidance instructions

B Thames Radar would obtain a clearance to transit the Elstree ATZ if it were necessary

C The pilot is responsible for traffic separation and for obtaining clearance into any CTR or ATZ

D Thames Radar are responsible for terrain clearance.

Questions and Answers
PAPER 1 *for the I M C Rating*

15 When flying over water using the ADF, coastal refraction may be kept to a minimum by:

A Using an NDB that is well inland

B Using the BFO facility

C Using an NDB that is on the coast

D Flying lower.

16 The operating limits of VOR radio navigation aids are specified by range and altitude. This is known as :

A Designated Operational Coverage (DOC) and is valid by day and night

B Designated Operational Coverage (DOC) and is valid by day only

C Delineated Operating Condition (DOC) and is valid by day only

D Delineated Operating Condition (DOC) and is valid by day and night.

17 You are flying towards a VOR on a Magnetic heading of 042°. The OBS is set to 035° and the CDI shows a 3 dot fly left deflection. Which radial is the aircraft currently on?

A 029°

B 221°

C 041°

D 209°.

18 When tuned to an ILS, full scale deflection of the CDI and glidepath needles will be seen when the aircraft has deviated from the centreline and glidepath by:

A 10° and 0.7° respectively

B 0.7° and 2.5° respectively

C 2.5° and 0.7° respectively

D 2.5° and 1° respectively.

19 It is standard practice to intercept an ILS glidepath from below to avoid following any false glidepath that may be present. The lowest false glidepath associated with a 3° ILS glidepath may be expected at:

A 6° above the horizon

B 8° above the horizon

C 10° above the horizon

D 12° above the horizon.

20 When the actual weather conditions at an aerodrome of intended landing include an RVR that is less than that required by the Aerodrome Operating Minima:

A The aeroplane must not descend below 1000ft QNH whilst within 2nm of the aerodrome

B The aircraft must not continue an approach to a runway, in respect of which a notified Instrument Approach Procedure (IAP) exists, by descending below 1000ft above the aerodrome

C The aeroplane must not descend below 1000ft above aerodrome elevation if the relevant RVR for that runway is at the time less than the calculated minimum for landing

D The aeroplane may make 1 approach to check the visibility before diverting.

21 Flying on limited panel you wish to turn from 200° to 350°. Which way should you turn, how long will it take (assume rate 1) and what will the compass indicate as you roll out of the turn?

A right; 50 seconds; 015°

B left; 50 seconds; 325°

C right; 50 seconds; 325°

D left; 170 seconds; 015°.

22 When reporting levels under routine procedures or when requested by ATC, pilots are required to state the current altimeter reading to the nearest 100ft to assist ATC in the verification of Mode C data transmitted by the aircraft transponder. ATC will instruct the pilot to switch off Mode C if the verification process reveals a difference between the level readout and the reported level of:

A 100ft

B 200ft

C 300ft

D 400ft.

23 When changing from a RIS to a RAS, which of the following statements are true?

A The controller becomes responsible for terrain clearance

B The aircraft must fly on a flight level

C Standard terrain clearance criteria no longer apply

D The pilot remains responsible for terrain clearance.

24 Flight into known icing conditions in an aircraft with no de-icing systems:

A Is quite acceptable as ice build up will enhance the aerodynamic profile of the aircraft

B May overload the aircraft and cause control problems

C Is acceptable provided the OAT is less than -5° C

D May improve control in pitch as the aircraft will be more stable.

25 Given the following data:

System minimum ILS: 200ft

System minimum ILS (localiser only): 250ft

OCH for ILS approach Runway 28 - 170ft aircraft Category A

OCH for ILS (localiser only) Runway 28 - 280ft aircraft Category A

Visual Manoeuvring (Circling) OCH - 510ft aircraft Category A

Determine the Decision Height/Minimum Descent Height for an IMC rated pilot in current practice:

	ILS ft	ILS (localiser only) ft
A	420	510
B	420	480
C	500	600
D	500	510

Questions and Answers for the IMC Rating — PAPER 1

FLIGHT PLAN

Latitude and longitude are given as an aid to identification, but where locations and facilities are marked on the chart, their charted positions should be used.

From	To	Safety Alt ft amsl	FL/Alt	TAS kt	Trk T	W/V	Hdg T	Varn	Hdg M	GS kt	Dist nm	Time min	ETA
CLACTON (514707N 0010744E)	LAMBOURNE (LAM) (513846N 0000906E)	1700	2400	120		140/10		3°W					
LAM	BOVINGDON (BNN) (514334N 0003259W)	2000	2400	120		150/18		4°W					
BNN	COMPTON (CPT) (512930N 0011311W)	2200	2400 ↗FL40	120		150/18		4°W					
CPT	CHILBOLTON (510830N 0012645W)	2300		120		170/15		5°W					
CHILBOLTON	COMPTON ABBAS (505803N 0020913W)	2200	Descent as required	120		170/15		5°W					
ALTERNATE											Totals		
COMPTON ABBAS	YEOVIL (505624N 0023938W)	2300	2500	120		180/10		5°W					

Note: Safety Altitude is derived from the higher of:

(i) the highest ground plus 1299 feet; or

(ii) the highest structure plus 1000 feet;

rounded up to the next 100 feet, within 5nm of track.

Questions and Answers
PAPER 1 *for the I M C Rating*

Reference Section
ANSWER PAPER 1

FLIGHT PLAN

Latitude and longitude are given as an aid to identification, but where locations and facilities are marked on the chart, their charted positions should be used.

From	To	Safety Alt ft amsl	FL/Alt	TAS kt	Trk T	W/V	Hdg T	Varn	Hdg M	GS kt	Dist nm	Time min	ETA
CLACTON (514707N 0010744E)	LAMBOURNE (LAM) (513846N 0000906E)	1700	2400	120	259	140/10	255	3°W	258	125	32.5	15.5	
LAM	BOVINGDON (BNN) (514334N 0003259W)	2000	2400	120	280	150/18	273	4°W	277	131	26.5	12	
BNN	COMPTON (CPT) (512930N 0011311W)	2200	FL40	120	240	150/18	231	4°W	235	118	28.5	14.5	
CPT	CHILBOLTON (510830N 0012645W)	2300	FL40	120	202	170/15	198	5°W	203	106	22.5	13	
CHILBOLTON	COMPTON ABBAS (N505803N 0020913W)	2200	Descent as required	120	249	170/15	242	5°W	247	116	28.5	15	
									Totals		138.5	70	
ALTERNATE													
COMPTON ABBAS	YEOVIL (505624N 0023938W)	2300	2500	120	265	180/10	260	5°W	265	118	19	9.5	

Note: Safety Altitude is derived from the higher of:

(i) the highest ground plus 1299 feet; or

(ii) the highest structure plus 1000 feet; rounded up to the next 100 feet, within 5nm of track.

1.11

Instrument Meteorlogical Conditions

ANSWER PAPER 1

1 A

The privileges of the IMC rating are detailed in the Air Navigation Order, and in rather more legible format in Civil Aviation Authority publication CAP 53 - The Private Pilot's Licence and Associated Ratings.

2 D

Refer to CAP 53, the period of validity is 25 months.

3 B

The UK Rules of the Air, rule 29 (Minimum height) and rule 30 (Quadrantal Rule and semi-circular Rule) apply.
The obstacle is at 2400ft amsl, plus the minimum obstacle clearance of 1000ft = 3400ft.
Thus 3400ft QNH is the lowest altitude useable.
The difference between QNH (993mb) and Standard pressure (1013mb) is 20mb. If 1mb is equivalent to 30ft; 20mb = a 600 ft height difference. As QNH is low (less than standard) this 600ft must be added to the lowest useable altitude, 3400ft + 600ft = 4000 ft.
Next determine the Magnetic track. With a True track of 162°, and variation of 6° east, Magnetic track is 156° (easterly variation is deducted from True track). In this sector (090° to 179°), cruising Flight Levels are chosen at ODD FL + 500. Above 4000ft, the next such quadrantal level is FL55.

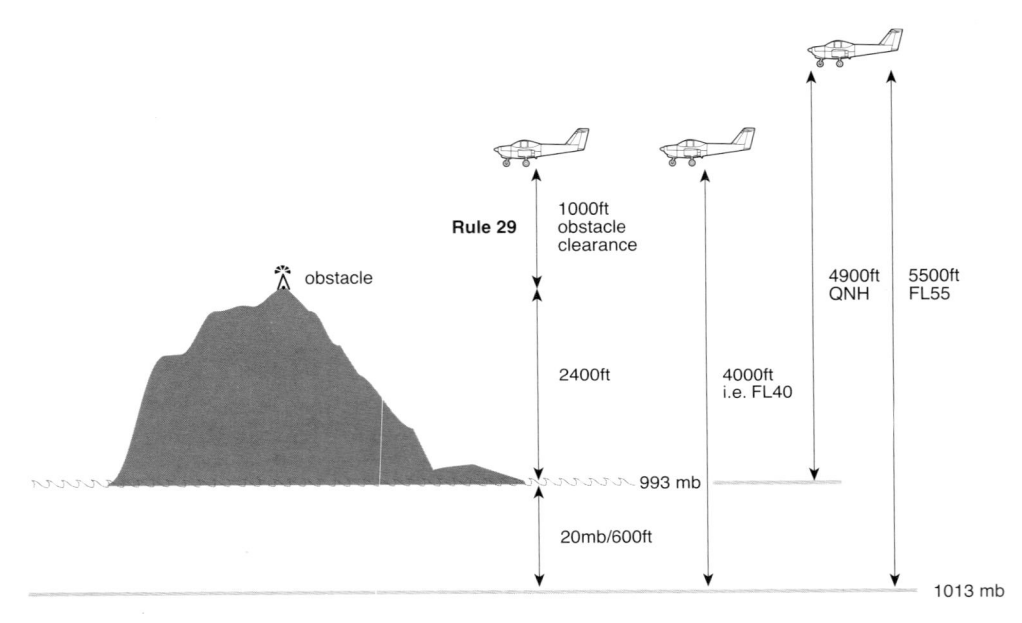

Further reference: The Private Pilot's Licence Course Book 2 (Air Law and Radiotelephony), Visual Flight Rules / Instrument Flight Rules section; The Private Pilot's Licence Course Book 3 (Navigation, Meteorology and Flight Planning) Vertical Navigation section.

4 C

From 1500 the visibility is forecast to drop to 1200 metres. This is below IMC limits. Thus plan to arrive before 1500 when the visibility is forecast to be 3000 metres.
Further reference: The Private Pilot's Licence Course Book 3 (Navigation, Meteorology and Flight Planning), Aviation Weather Reports and Forecasts section; IMC rated pilot visibility limits for landing – AIP AD 1.1.2.

5 D

Bright runway lighting in a featureless area will lead the pilot into thinking that the runway is closer than it really is. Thus it is likely that the descent will be started too soon and the pilot may become too low on the approach and undershoot the runway.

Reference Section

ANSWER PAPER 1

6 C

From the flight plan, track (T) should be 240°. Apply the variation for the area of 4°W remembering that 'West is Best' (i.e. add variation to True track); therefore track Magnetic is 244° (M).
Further reference: The Private Pilot's Licence Course Book 3 (Navigation, Meteorology and Flight Planning), Aeronautical Maps section.

7 B

This figure is taken from the flight plan. As a gross error check, note that the angle between wind and track gives a headwind.
Further reference: The Private Pilot's Licence Course Book 3 (Navigation, Meteorology and Flight Planning), Navigation Principles 1 section.

8 B

The Safety Altitude on this leg is 2300ft (taken from the flight plan). The magnetic track on this leg is 207°(M), (True track 202° + varn 5°W). In this sector of the quadrantal rule (180° to 279°), even Flight Levels are used. As QNH is 1013mb, the next even FL can be used - FL40.
Further reference: The Private Pilot's Licence Course Book 2 (Air Law and Radiotelephony), Visual Flight Rules / Instrument Flight Rules section; The Private Pilot's Licence Course Book 3 (Navigation, Meteorology and Flight Planning) Vertical Navigation section.

9 C

Total the leg distances on the flight plan, the answer is 138.5nm.
Further reference: The Private Pilot's Licence Course Book 3 (Navigation, Meteorology and Flight Planning), Navigation Principles 1 section.

10 C

Taken from the flight plan.
Further reference: The Private Pilot's Licence Course Book 3 (Navigation, Meteorology and Flight Planning), Navigation Principles 1 section.

11 A

The total 'en-route' time from the flight plan is 76·5 minutes (1:16·5). Set course time 1433, plus 'en-route' time of 1 hour 16·5 minutes = ETA 1549·5.
The closest answer to this figure is answer A: 1549.

12 D

Calculate fuel burns:
Clacton - Compton Abbas   1 hr 10mins @ 30lt/hr = **35** litres
Compton Abbas - Yeovil   9·5mins @ 30lt/hr =   **5** litres
Holding   45mins @ 30lt/hr = **23** litres
Complete the table by adding up all quantities:
10 + **35** + 15 + **5** + **23** + 10 + 30. Total fuel required = 128 litres.

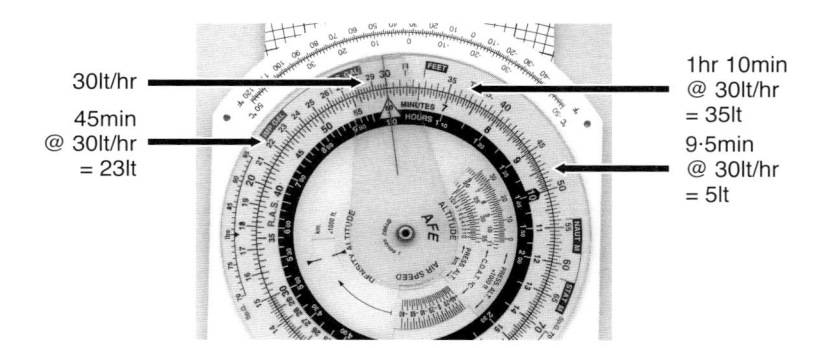

30lt/hr

45min @ 30lt/hr = 23lt

1hr 10min @ 30lt/hr = 35lt

9·5min @ 30lt/hr = 5lt

Further reference: The Private Pilot's Licence Course Book 3 (Navigation, Meteorolgy and Flight Planning), Fuel Planning and Performance sections.

Instrument Meteorlogical Conditions
ANSWER PAPER 1

13 A
The altimeter setting regions can be found on the ICAO 1:500,000 Southern England chart, and also in the UK AIP ENR 1.7.
Further reference: The Private Pilot's Licence Course Book 2 (Air Law and Radiotelephony), Altimeter Setting Procedures section.

14 C
The Radar Information Service is described in the UK AIP ENR 1.6.1 and also in various CAA literature, such as the 'General Aviation Safety Sense' leaflets. With respect to this specific question, regardless of receiving an RIS, the pilot remains responsible for terrain clearance and for negotiating clearances through ATZs if they are not under the control of the unit he is talking to.

15 C
In coastal areas the different radio energy absorption properties of land and water result in refraction of NDB transmissions. This error is most marked when transmissions cross the coast at an oblique angle or the NDB is located away from the coastline. Thus to minimise coastal refraction use an NDB close to the coast when operating the aircraft over water.

16 A
The UK AIP GEN 3 refers.

17 D
Remember, a radial is a bearing from the VOR. If the OBS is set to 035°, and the CDI is showing a 3 dot fly left indication (1 dot = 2°), then the aircraft's actual QDM to the VOR is 029°. The reciprocal of this (to turn the QDM into a QDR, a radial) is 029 + 180 = 209°.
Note: the heading has nothing to do with the bearing of the aircraft relative to the VOR.

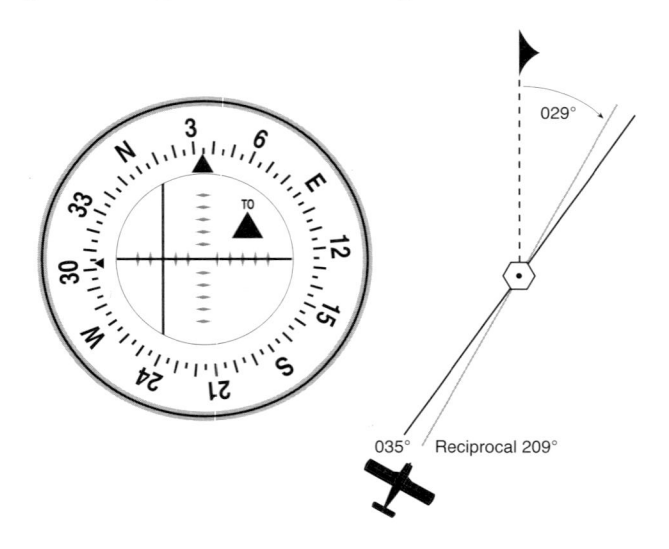

18 C
When an ILS is selected, the localiser needle scale deflection is at the rate of 0·5°/dot and glidepath needle scale deflection is at the rate of 0·14°/dot. Therefore full scale deflections are (5 X 0·5°) = 2.5° for the localiser and (5 X 0·14°) = 0.7° for the glidepath.

19 A
The first false glidepath occurs at 6° above the horizon, double the actual glidepath angle of 3°. There is usually a pink AIC current which details this phenomena.

20 B
This stipulation is contained within the Air Navigation Order, and also detailed within the UK AIP AD1.1.2, where it is known as 'The Approach Ban'.

Reference Section

ANSWER PAPER 1

21 C

To turn from 200° to 350° requires a right turn (shortest direction). You are turning through 150° @ 3°/sec (a rate 1 turn) so 150 ÷ 3 = 50 sec. Turning toward north the needle will be sluggish so roll out early, by approximately 25°. Therefore stop the turn when compass shows 325°.

Further reference: The Private Pilot's Licence Course Book 3 (Navigation, Meteorolgy and Flight Planning), Special Navigational Situations; The Private Pilot's Licence Course Book 1 (Flying Training), Exercise 9 - Turning.

22 B

UK AIP ENR 1.6 refers.

23 D

Under RIS and RAS the pilot is responsible for terrain clearance.

Further reference: The Private Pilot's Licence Course Book 2 (Air Law and RT), En-route Procedures.

24 B

Aircraft without de-icing systems are not approved for flight in known icing conditions. Without a de-icing system ice build up will not be halted unless the aircraft can return to a level or area where air temperature is above 0°C.

25 C

UK AIP AD 1.1.2 refers.

System minimum ILS Cat 1 approach 200ft; system minimum ILS (localiser only) is 250ft. The OCH on the ILS Cat 1 approach is 170ft, the ILS (localiser only) approach is a non-precision approach.

a) System minimum is higher than OCH, so use system minimum as basis for calculation.

System Minimum	200ft
Add IMC Allowance	200ft
Add Position Error Correction	50ft
Total	450ft

Recommended minimum Decision Height (DH) for a precision approach by an IMC rated pilot is 500ft, as this is higher than 450ft use 500ft as the Decision Height for the ILS approach.

b) OCH is higher of the two figures so use OCH as basis for calculation.

OCH	280ft
Add IMC Allowance	200ft
(note: Position Error Correction is not needed for non-precision approach)	
Total	480ft

The recommended Minimum Descent Height (MDH) for non-precision approach by an IMC rated pilot is 600ft, as this is higher than 480ft use 600ft as Minimum Descent Height for the ILS (localiser only) approach.

Instrument Meteorlogical Conditions
ANSWER PAPER 1

Questions and Answers
for the IMC Rating **PAPER 2**

Instructions

1. Time allowed 2 hours.

2. Twenty five multi-choice questions each carrying 4 marks. Marks are not deducted for wrong answers. The pass mark is 72% (i.e. 18 questions or more must be answered correctly).

3. Unless otherwise specified, the questions relate to a UK licenced pilot, operating a UK registered aircraft in UK airspace.

4. Read each question carefully as there is only one answer which is correct.

5. Remember examination technique, you are advised to pass over questions that seem difficult at first sight and return to them when you have answered the others.

Questions and Answers

for the IMC Rating **PAPER 2**

1 You pass your IMC rating flight test on 16th September 1998 and the rating is subsequently issued on 30th September 1998. A revalidation flight test will be required on:

A 29th September 2000

B 15th September 2000

C 29th October 2000

D 15th October 2000.

2 The holder of a valid IMC rating can request clearance in a 'class A' airspace control zone when the visibility is less than 10km. Such a clearance would be:

A An IFR clearance which the pilot can accept

B A Special VFR clearance, which the ATC unit is obliged to offer

C A Special VFR clearance, which is offered at the discretion of the ATC unit

D A IMC VFR clearance, accepted at the pilot's discretion.

3 You are flying at FL65, Regional QNH993, over terrain with a maximum elevation of 2850ft amsl. If you descend to FL45 will you be able to maintain the minimum obstacle clearance required for IFR flight (assume 1mb = 30ft)?

A No, by 1549ft

B No, by 249ft

C Yes, by 249ft

D Yes, by 1549ft.

4 The forecast for your intended destination reads:
040600Z 040716 07005KT 1500 BR SCT250 BECMG 1012 2500
Which of the following statements is correct:

A Conditions will remain within IMC rating limits throughout the period

B Conditions will remain below IMC rating limits throughout the period

C You should plan to arrive at your destination after 1200 hrs

D You should plan to arrive at your destination prior to 1200 hrs.

5 An illusion of pitching down may be experienced by the pilot when the aeroplane is subject to:

A Rapid deceleration

B Rapid acceleration

C Rapid throttle opening

D A transition from straight and level flight to a climb.

Questions and Answers

PAPER 2 *for the I M C Rating*

Complete the attached flight plan using an ICAO 1:500,000 chart for Southern England, then answer questions 6-13

6 What is the appropriate Quadrantal Level for the leg from YEOVIL to LYNEHAM assuming a QNH of 1013mb?

A FL40

B FL45

C FL50

D FL55.

7 What is the Magnetic heading between LYNEHAM and COMPTON?

A 097°

B 101°

C 104°

D 087°.

8 What is the Magnetic track between CRANFIELD and DEENTHORPE?

A 356°

B 006°

C 342°

D 352°.

9 What is the Minimum Safety Altitude between CRANFIELD and DEENTHORPE?

A 1000ft

B 1500ft

C 2700ft

D 1900ft.

10 What is the total distance from EXETER to DEENTHORPE?

A 170nm

B 195nm

C 178½nm

D 183nm.

11 What is the total time required for the flight from EXETER to DEENTHORPE?

A 80·5mins

B 85·5mins

C 101mins

D 105mins.

12 What is the minimum fuel uplift required for this flight (to the nearest litre) given that:

Start, Taxy and Take-off and climb	2imp gal
Exeter to Deenthorpe @ 8imp gal/hr	
Approach and Missed Approach	3imp gal
Divert Deenthorpe - Cranfield @ 8imp gal/hr	
Approach and Landing	2imp gal
Holding 45mins @ 8imp gal/hr	
Reserve	8imp gal
Fuel in tank prior to refuelling	6imp gal

A 132lt

B 125lt

C 141lt

D 147lt

---

13 With reference to the Yeovilton MATZ which statement is correct:

A It has a circle of 5nm radius extending from sea level to 3000ft amsl. The contact frequency is 127.350

B It has a circle of 5nm radius extending from 75ft amsl to 3000ft aal. The contact frequency is 127.350

C It has a circle of 2nm radius extending from 75ft amsl to 3000ft aal. The contact frequency is 127.350

D It has a circle of 5nm radius extending from 75ft amsl to 3000ft aal. The contact frequency is 111.900.

---

14 Whilst operating over a built up area which lies within a Control Zone (CTR) in accordance with a Special VFR clearance, the aircraft must be flown to ensure that:

A It must be able to glide clear of the built up area if it suffers an engine failure and in any event shall not fly closer than 500ft to any vehicle, vessel, person or structure

B It must be at least 1500ft above the highest fixed object within 2000ft of the aircraft

C It must be at least 2000ft above the highest fixed object within 1500ft of the aircraft

D It must remain at 1500ft except for the purpose of take-off and landing.

---

15 An NDB bears 045° relative. Your HDG is 340° (M). Assuming variation is 5°W, what is the true bearing of the aircraft from the NDB?

A 025°

B 020°

C 200°

D 205°.

Questions and Answers
PAPER 2 *for the I M C Rating*

16 Study the VOR display and choose the correct response:

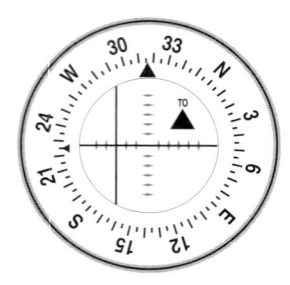

A The aeroplane is on the 321° radial and a left turn is required to regain track

B The aeroplane is on the 311° radial and a left turn is required to regain track

C The aeroplane is on the 131° radial and a left turn is required to regain track

D The aeroplane is on the 141° radial and a right turn is required to regain track.

17 A 2 dot CDI deflection at 45nm from the VOR would indicate a track error of:

A 4nm

B 3nm

C 2nm

D 1nm.

18 In relation to the aircraft position and ILS instrument presentation shown below (assume the CDI is tuned to the ILS for the runway depicted), select the correct response:

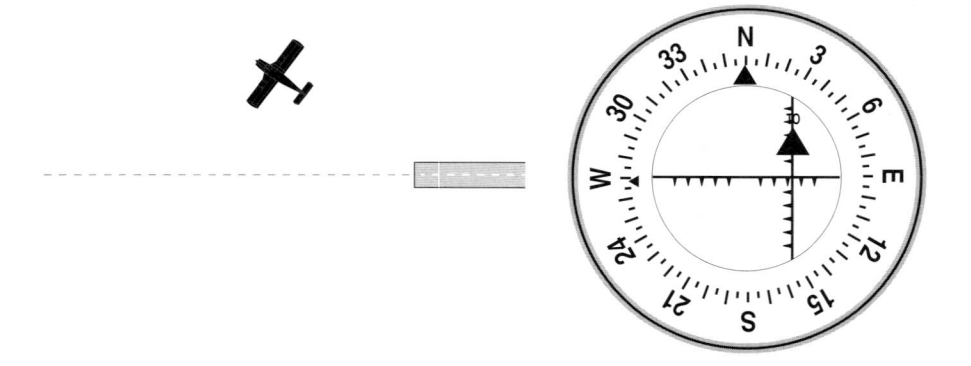

A The CDI will show a fly right indication, regardless of the OBS selected

B With the CDI centred, the correct QDM to the runway threshold will be displayed on the OBS

C The instrument should be showing a 'From' indication

D The CDI needle will centre when the correct localiser QDM is selected.

19 Cockpit indications of passage over the Middle Marker are:

A An aural series of low pitch dashes transmitted at 6 per second and a synchronised blue light

B An aural series of low pitch dots and dashes transmitted at 2 per second and a synchronised blue light

C An aural series of medium pitch dots and dashes transmitted at 6 per second and a synchronised orange light

D An aural series of medium pitch dots and dashes transmitted at 6 per second and a synchronised white light.

20 Decision Height is defined as:

A The height in a non-precision approach below which descent may not be made without the required visual reference for landing

B The point in a precision approach at or before which the prescribed missed approach procedure must be initiated in order to ensure that the minimum obstacle clearance is not infringed

C The height in a precision approach at which a missed approach must be initiated if the required visual reference to continue the approach has not been established

D The height in a non-precision approach at which a missed approach must be initiated if the required visual reference to continue the approach has not been established.

21 As you commence a descent you become aware that the pitot tube has become blocked by ice. During the descent the altimeter will:

A overread

B underread

C read correctly

D vary between over and under reading.

22 In relation to radio contact with an ATC unit to request a RAS or RIS service, the pilot must read-back:

A The ATC unit's callsign

B Whether or not the aircraft is identified

C Exact details of conflicting traffic reported to the aircraft

D The type of radar service offered.

Questions and Answers
PAPER 2 *for the I M C Rating*

Refer to the AIP extract below

Lands End VOR/DME (5.5°W - 1996)	LND	114.20 MHz (Ch 89X)	H24	500811N 0053813W	800 ft amsl	DOC 200 nm/50000 ft (300 nm/ 70000 ft in Sector 234°-009°M).

23 You intend to track 322° from the Lands End VOR. Up to what range from the VOR may you expect to receive a reliable signal assuming 'line of sight' considerations do not apply:

A 300nm

B 200nm

C 100nm

D 40nm.

24 Which of the following may be expected if ice accumulation causes the aircraft centre of gravity to move aft of the maximum limit?

A Increased longitudinal stability

B A tendency to dive when reducing power

C Decreased longitudinal stability

D Increased range.

25 Given the following data:
VOR approach system minima 300ft.
OCH for VOR approach Runway 35 - 420ft aircraft Category A
Visual Manoeuvring (Circling) OCH - 550ft aircraft Category A
You intend to fly the VOR approach to Runway 35, then circle to land on runway 26.
The Minimum Descent Height (MDH) and Visual Manoeuvring (Circling) OCH you should use are:

A 550ft; 550ft respectively

B 670ft; 550ft respectively

C 620ft; 550ft respectively

D 670ft; 400ft respectively.

Questions and Answers for the IMC Rating — PAPER 2

FLIGHT PLAN

Latitude and longitude are given as an aid to identification, but where locations and facilities are marked on the chart, their charted positions should be used.

From	To	Safety Alt ft amsl	FL/Alt	TAS kt	Trk T	W/V	Varn	Hdg T	Hdg M	GS kt	Dist nm	Time min	ETA
EXETER (504404N 0032450W)	YEOVIL (YVL) (5056627N 0023952W)	2600	FL50	105		190/25	5°W						
YVL	LYNEHAM (LA) (513030N 0020018W)	2300		105		200/20	5°W						
LA	COMPTON (CPT) (512930N 0011311W)	2200	FL55 ↙	105		230/20	5°W						
CPT	CRANFIELD (CFD) (520427N 0003639W)	2200	2800	105		260/25	5°W						
CFD	DEENTHORPE (523024N 0003524W)		Descent as required	105		260/25	5°W						
ALTERNATE										Totals			
DEENTHORPE	CRANFIELD (520420N 0003700W)	1900	2500	105		260/25	5°W						

Note: Safety Altitude is derived from the higher of:

(i) the highest ground plus 1299 feet; or

(ii) the highest structure plus 1000 feet; rounded up to the next 100 feet, within 5nm of track.

Questions and Answers
PAPER 2 *for the IMC Rating*

Questions and Answers
PAPER 2 *for the IMC Rating*

Reference Section
ANSWER PAPER 2

FLIGHT PLAN

Latitude and longitude are given as an aid to identification, but where locations and facilities are marked on the chart, their charted positions should be used.

From	To	Safety Alt ft amsl	FL/Alt	TAS kt	Trk T	W/V	Hdg T	Varn	Hdg M	GS kt	Dist nm	Time min	ETA
EXETER (504404N 0032450W)	YEOVIL (YVL) (505627N 0023952W)	2600	FL50	105	067	190/25	079	5°W	084	116	31	16	
YVL	LYNEHAM (LA) (513030N 0020018W)	2300	FL50	105	035	200/20	038	5°W	043	124	42	20	
LA	COMPTON (CPT) (512930N 0011311W)	2200	FL55	105	092	230/20	099	5°W	104	120	29.5	14.5	
CPT	CRANFIELD (CFD) (520427N 0003639W)	2200	2800	105	033	260/25	023	5°W	028	121	41.5	21	
CFD	DEENTHORPE (523024N 0003524W)	1900	Descent as required	105	001	260/25	347	5°W	352	107	26	14	
ALTERNATE										Totals	170	85.5	
DEENTHORPE	CRANFIELD (520420N 0003700W)	1900	2500	105	181	260/25	195	5°W	200	98	26	16	

Note: Safety Altitude is derived from the higher of:

(i) the highest ground plus 1299 feet; or

(ii) the highest structure plus 1000 feet; rounded up to the next 100 feet, within 5nm of track.

Instrument Meteorlogical Conditions

ANSWER PAPER 2

1 D

Refer to CAP 53. The period of validity is 25 months from the date of the successful flight test.

2 C

See ENR 1.2 of the UK AIP
Further reference: The Private Pilot's Licence Course Book 2 (Air Law and Radiotelephony), Visual Flight Rules / Instrument Flight Rules section.

3 B

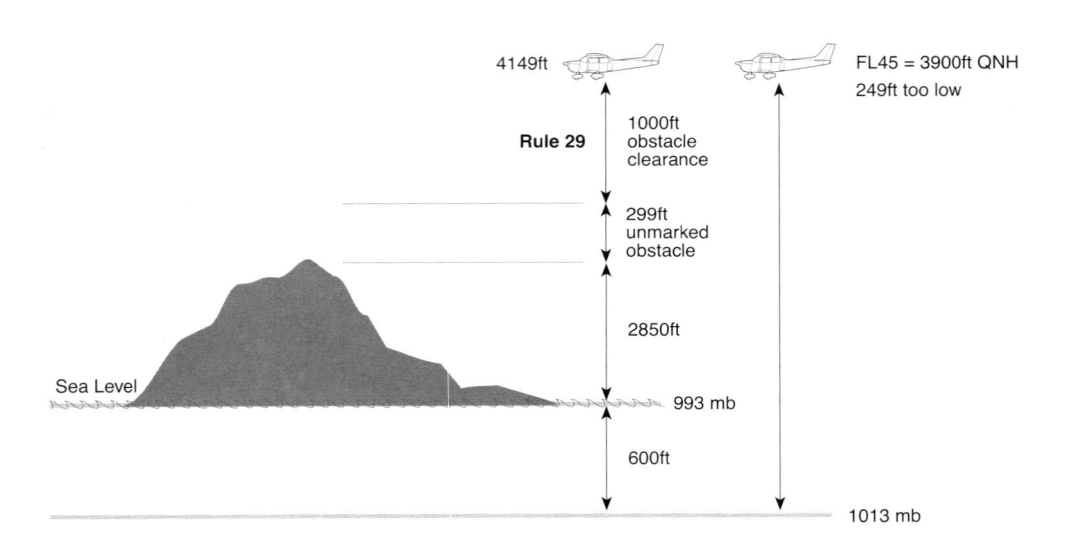

[Diagram showing aircraft at 4149ft with Rule 29 clearances: 1000ft obstacle clearance, 299ft unmarked obstacle, 2850ft terrain, 993 mb at sea level, 600ft to 1013 mb. Second aircraft at FL45 = 3900ft QNH, 249ft too low.]

The UK Rules of the Air. Rules 29 and 30 apply.

Difference between QNH and Standard Pressure is 20mb. This equates (at 1mb = 30ft) to 600ft. As QNH is low, altimeter will read high when set to 1013mb. So FL45 equates to 3900ft QNH. As 4149ft is the required safety altitude (2850ft terrain + 299ft possible obstacle + 1000ft safety margin) the aircraft is 249ft too low.
Further reference: The Private Pilot's Licence Course Book 2 (Air Law and Radiotelephony), Visual Flight Rules / Instrument Flight Rules section; The Private Pilot's Licence Course Book 3 (Navigation, Meteorology and Flight Planning) Vertical Navigation section.

4 C

Refer to Air Navigation Order - Schedule 8 - IMC rating privileges (also in CAP53). According to the forecast, by 1200hrs the visibility should be in excess of the minimum required by an IMC rated pilot (which is 1800m for landing).
Further reference: The Private Pilot's Licence Course Book 3 (Navigation, Meteorology and Flight Planning), Aviation Weather Reports and Forecasts section; IMC rated pilot visibility limits for landing - AIP AD 1.1.2.

5 A

The diagram shows that a deceleration force operates similarly to the weight force of a

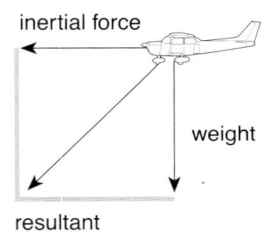

[Diagram showing aircraft with inertial force (horizontal), weight (vertical), and resultant vector.]

descending aircraft. Without visual references the pilot may easily interpret a deceleration as a pitch down.

6 C

From the flight plan, the TRK (T) from Yeovil to Lyneham is 035°; + Var 5°W = TRK (M) 040°. In this sector (000 - 089) ODD FLs apply, and so FL50 is used.
Further reference: The Private Pilot's Licence Course Book 2 (Air Law and Radiotelephony), Visual Flight Rules / Instrument Flight Rules section; The Private Pilot's Licence Course Book 3 (Navigation, Meteorology and Flight Planning) Vertical Navigation section.

7 C

The Magnetic heading can be taken from the completed flight plan. As a gross error check, note that with the wind to the right of track, the aircraft must head slightly into wind to maintain track. Don't forget to add the variation of 5° W to the calculated True heading.
Further reference: The Private Pilot's Licence Course Book 3 (Navigation, Meteorology and Flight Planning), Navigation Principles 1 section.

8 B

From the completed flight plan, Track (T) between CFD and Deenethorpe is 001°. Apply the variation for the area 5°W (remembering that 'West is best'), so 001 + 005 = track (M) of 006.
Further reference: The Private Pilot's Licence Course Book 3 (Navigation, Meteorology and Flight Planning), Aeronautical Maps section.

9 D

Taken from the completed flight plan, calculated as below.

On the relevant ICAO 1:500,000 Southern England map, the highest point within 5nm of track is the spot height of 561ft, 4·5nm south-west of Cranfield.

Thus:

Highest terrain = spot height	561ft
+ Allowance for obstacles	299ft
=	860ft
Round up to	900ft
+ safety margin	1000ft
= Safety Altitude	1900ft

Further reference: The Private Pilot's Licence Course Book 3 (Navigation, Meteorology and Flight Planning) Vertical Navigation section.

10 A

From the completed flight plan, add up leg distances = 170nm.
(note: do NOT include the diversion. Remember, read the question carefully).

11 B

From the completed flight plan add up times = 85·5 minutes.
(note: do NOT include the diversion. Remember, read the question carefully).

Instrument Meteorlogical Conditions

ANSWER PAPER 2

12 A

Calculate fuel burns with the Flight Computer set to the fuel consumption of 8 imperial gallons per hour:

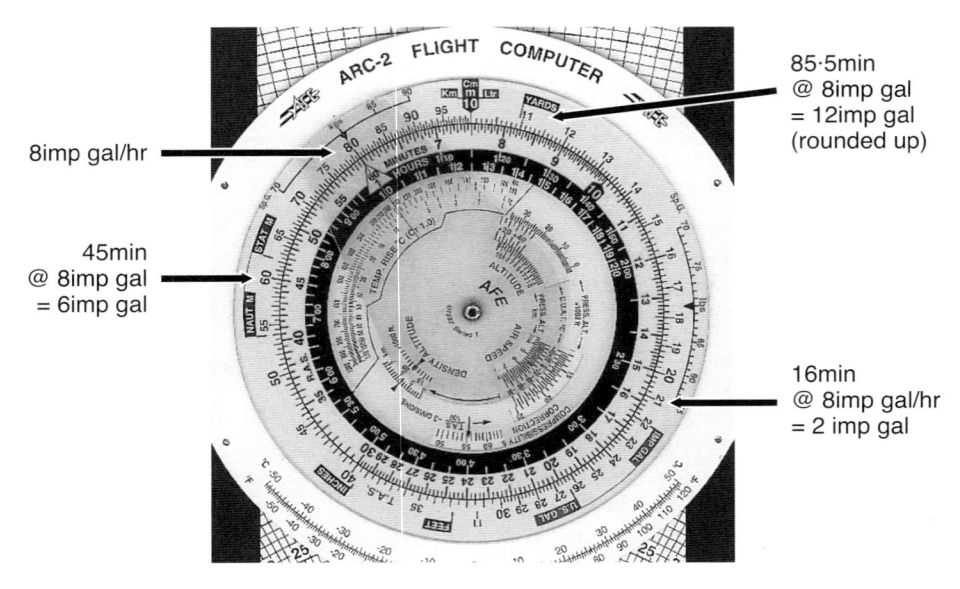

- 8imp gal/hr
- 45min @ 8imp gal = 6imp gal
- 85·5min @ 8imp gal = 12imp gal (rounded up)
- 16min @ 8imp gal/hr = 2 imp gal

Exeter to Deenthorpe 1hr 25·5mins @ 8imp gal /hr = 12imp gal
Deenthorpe to Cranfield   16mins @ 8imp gal /hr = 2imp gal
Holding   45mins @ 8imp gal /hr = 6imp gal

Complete the table 2 + **12** + 3 + **2** + 2 + 6 + 8 = 35
(all figures are rounded up to the nearest imp gal)

Note that 6 imp gal are already in the tanks.
Consequently, fuel uplift required is 35 - 6 = 29.

Minimum fuel uplift required = 29 imp gal. convert to 132 litres.
Further reference: The Private Pilot's Licence Course Book 3 (Navigation, Meteorolgy and Flight Planning), Fuel Planning and Performance sections.

13 B

Dimensions of a MATZ are detailed in the UK AIP ENR 2.2, the radio frequency can be found on the map.
Further reference: The Private Pilot's Licence Course Book 2 (Air Law and Radiotelephony), Rules of the Air and Air Traffic Control.

14 A

UK Rules of the Air - Rule 5 (Low Flying). When in receipt of a SVFR clearance you are exempt from the '1500ft' rule in relation to a congested area, but must still be able to glide clear. The '500ft' rule still applies.
Further reference: The Private Pilot's Licence Course Book 2 (Air Law and Radiotelephony), Rules of the Air and Air Traffic Control.

15 C

HDG	340
RBI	+ 045
	385
	- 360
QDM (to NDB)	= 025
	+ 180
QDR (from NDB)	= 205
(Variation)	- 5
QTE (true)	200°

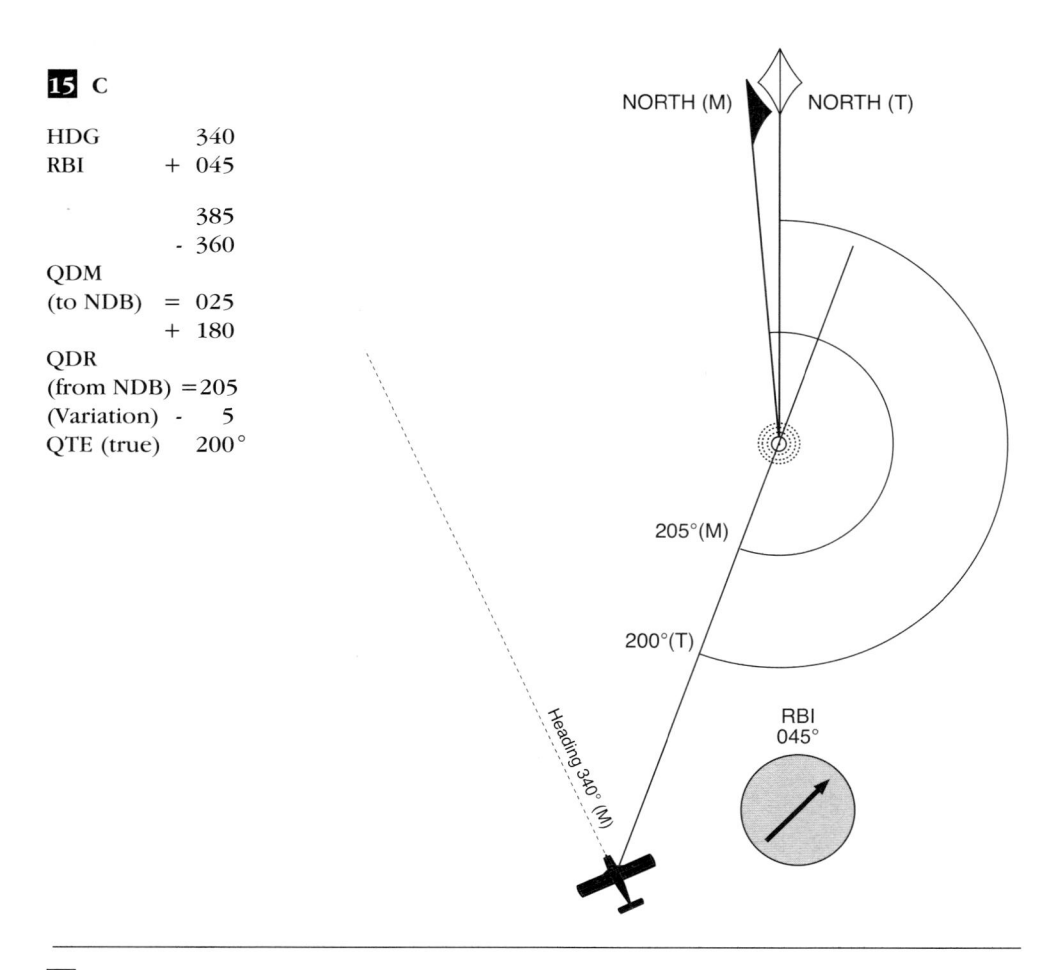

16 C

The aircraft is 5° right of the 316 QDM, in other words it is on the 311 QDM. Subtract 180° to get the radial from the beacon (the QDR) of 131°

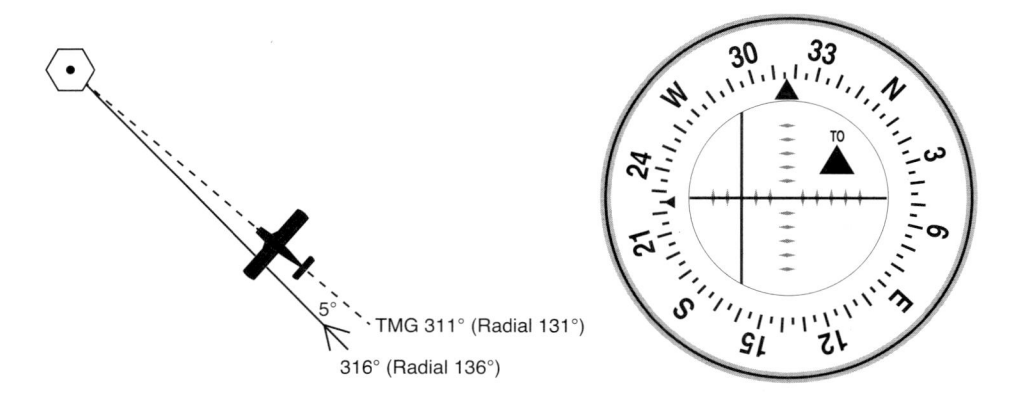

17 B

Use 1 in 60 rule.

1° off track at 60nm = 1nm off-track.
1° off track at 45nm = 0·75nm off-track.

2 dots CDI deflection = 4°

4 x 0·75nm = 3nm off-track.

Instrument Meteorlogical Conditions

ANSWER PAPER 2

18 A

The CDI needle is not affected by the OBS selected once an ILS localiser has been tuned. It will only display a fly left/right indication in respect of the Final Approach Track QDM (illustrated on the diagram as the extended centreline). The needle deflection is only affected by displacement left or right of the ILS localiser centreline.

19 C

The ILS marker characteristics are:

Marker	Instrument Colour	Audio Indication
Outer marker	Blue	2 dashes/sec
Middle marker	Orange	dot/dashes @ 6 per second
Inner marker	White	6 dots/sec.

20 C

'Decision Height' applies to a precision approach only, and relates to visual sighting of the required visual reference (normally a stated number of runway/approach lights).

Ref: UK AIP AD 1.1.2.

21 C

The altimeter is not connected to the pitot source! The altimeter relies on static pressure only, not pitot pressure.

22 D

Further reference: The Private Pilot's Licence Course Book 2 (Air Law and Radiotelephony), En-Route Procedures.

23 A

Check the DOC for the Lands End VOR on the AIP extract. Within the sector 234° - 009° (M) the DOC is 300nm.

24 C

With an aft C of G the tailplane has a shortened moment arm, this leads to reduced pitch (or longitudinal) stability.

25 C

UK AIP AD 1.1.2 refers.

The system minima for a VOR Approach is: 300ft
OCH is: 420ft

As OCH is higher of the two figures, OCH is used as the basis for MDH calculation.

OCH 420ft
IMC Allowance 200ft

So MDH = 620ft

This is higher than absolute minima for an IMC rated pilot flying a non-precision approach (600ft) and so becomes the MDH. Remember, for a non-precision approach, altimeter Position Error Correction does not need to be added.

Visual Manoeuvring (Circling) OCH is 550ft as stated. No allowances need to be added to this figure.

Questions and Answers for the IMC Rating **PAPER 3**

Instructions

1. Time allowed 2 hours.

2. Twenty five multi-choice questions each carrying 4 marks. Marks are not deducted for wrong answers. The pass mark is 72% (i.e. 18 questions or more must be answered correctly).

3. Unless otherwise specified, the questions relate to a UK licenced pilot, operating a UK registered aircraft in UK airspace.

4. Read each question carefully as there is only one answer which is correct.

5. Remember examination technique, you are advised to pass over questions that seem difficult at first sight and return to them when you have answered the others.

Questions and Answers for the IMC Rating — PAPER 3

1 A Private Pilot holding a valid IMC rating may exercise the privileges of the rating:

A Throughout Europe

B Within the UK territorial airspace, and in Channel Islands and Isle of Man airspace

C World-wide

D Only within mainland UK.

2 The holder of an IMC rating requires a minimum visibility of ...... for take-off and landing, whilst a minimum visibility of ...... is required when flying in accordance with a Special VFR clearance. The respective visibilities are:

A 1800m; 10km

B 1800m; 3km

C 1500m; 3km

D 1500m; 10km.

3 The highest ground within 5nm of the aircraft is 3200ft amsl. If you elect to cruise at FL40 when the Regional QNH is 985mb, which of the following statements is correct:

A You will not be complying with the IFR but you will remain above the ground

B You will not be complying with the IFR and there will be a risk of striking the ground

C You will be complying with the IFR and there will be a risk of striking the ground

D You will be complying with the IFR and you will remain above the ground.

4 The forecast for your intended destination reads:
170830Z 171019 23015KT 6000 RA BKN012 OVC018 BECMG 1619 3000 +RA OVC003
Assuming that only an NDB/DME approach is published for the airfield, which of the following statements is correct?

A Conditions will remain within IMC rating limits throughout the period

B Conditions will remain below IMC rating limits throughout the period

C You should plan to arrive at your destination prior to 1600hrs

D You should plan to arrive at your destination after 1600hrs.

5 When flying in and out of cloud with limited flight visibility the pilot should:

A Rely on seat of the pants (somatosensory) information

B Look vertically down at the ground to judge aircraft attitude

C Believe the aircraft instruments

D Move the head from side to side whilst checking aircraft attitude against the cloud tops.

Questions and Answers

PAPER 3 *for the I M C Rating*

Complete the attached flight plan using an ICAO 1:500,000 chart for Southern England then answer questions 6-13

6 What is the Magnetic track between HAVERFORDWEST and BRECON?

A 102°

B 091°

C 089°

D 083°.

7 What is the Magnetic heading between GLOUCESTERSHIRE and DAVENTRY?

A 072°

B 066°

C 055°

D 060°.

8 What is the Minimum Safe Altitude between NETHERTHORPE and EAST MIDLANDS?

A 1400ft

B 1500ft

C 1700ft

D 2000ft.

9 What is the leg time between GAMSTON and NETHERTHORPE?

A 3mins

B 5mins

C 7mins

D 9mins.

10 What is the total distance from HAVERFORDWEST to NETHERTHORPE?

A 223km

B 234km

C 223nm

D 234nm.

11 You are overhead DAVENTRY at 0945. Based on flight plan time what is your ETA for NETHERTHORPE?

A 1025

B 1029

C 1032

D 1039.

12 What is the minimum fuel required for this flight (to the nearest lb. or imp gal):

Start, Taxy and Take-off and climb	15lb
Haverfordwest to Netherthorpe @ 65lb/hr	
Approach and Missed Approach	22lb
Divert Netherthorpe to East Midlands @ 65lb/hr	
Approach and Landing	15lb
Hold 45mins @ 65lb/hr	
Reserve	65lb

SG of fuel .72

A   38imp gal

B   42imp gal

C   45imp gal

D   48imp gal.

13 Whilst routing between GLOUCESTERSHIRE and DAVENTRY, Lower Airspace Radar Service may be obtained from:

A   Gloucestershire Radar 120.970

B   Birmingham Radar 118.050

C   Brize Radar 134.300

D   Filton Radar 122.720.

14 Given the data below, how much fuel must be burnt off to ensure that the aircraft will be able to obey the Maximum Landing Weight (MLW) limitation on arrival at destination:

Basic Aircraft Weight	1525lb.
Fuel loaded prior to departure 50US gal (SG .72)	
Pilot	185lb.
Passengers	350lb.
Baggage	40lb.
Maximum Take-Off Weight	2400lb.
Maximum Landing Weight	2300lb.

A   19US Gal

B   9US Gal

C   14·5US Gal

D   16·5US Gal.

15 Within the UK the range promulgated for an NDB is valid:

A   By day and by night

B   By day and night only in summer

C   By day only

D   Between 0600 and 1800 UTC daily.

16 Which of the following OBS/CDI combinations confirms that your aircraft is located within the 180 - 269° sector relative to the VOR?

A 270° TO + fly right

B 270° TO + fly left

C 090° TO + fly right

D 090° TO + fly left.

17 You receive the following ATC clearance "Right turn after departure, to exit the zone at Congleton not above 1500ft QNH, VFR". Assuming that Congleton is a 'congested area' which of the following statements is true?

A The pilot is not absolved from any of the provisions of Rule 5 (The Low Flying Rules)

B The pilot is absolved from the '1500ft' provision of Rule 5 (The Low Flying Rules)

C The pilot is obliged to fly over Congleton at 1500ft QNH, responsibility of complying with Rule 5 (The Low Flying Rules) rests with ATC in this instance

D The pilot can assume that Congleton is an area notified for exemption from Rule 5 (The Low Flying Rules).

18 The localiser of a UK ILS provides coverage through an arc of ... at the following distances:

A 35° up to 25nm

B 25° up to 10nm

C 15° up to 25nm

D 10° up to 25nm.

19 A DME associated with an ILS will:

A Have a greater transmitter power than a DME associated with a VOR

B Give a zero range indication at Decision Height

C Give a zero range indication as the aeroplane overflies the transmitter

D Give a zero range indication with respect to the threshold of the runway.

20 The Obstacle Clearance Height (OCH) for an NDB/DME approach is 350ft. The system minimum for a NDB/DME approach is 300ft. Calculate the recommended Minimum Descent Height (MDH) to be observed by an IMC rated pilot in current flying practice flying in a Category A aeroplane:

A 650ft

B 500ft

C 400ft

D 600ft.

21 As part of the pre-flight instrument checks the pilot should note that whilst the aircraft is manoeuvred in left and right turns whilst taxying:

A The attitude indicator should have no tendency to show any bank or pitch indications

B The attitude indicator should show roll in the same direction as the aircraft turns

C The turn co-ordinator should show roll in the opposite direction to the turn

D The direction indicator should show a decrease of heading when the aeroplane is turned to the right.

22 As an IMC rated Private Pilot you plan to transit an area of Class D airspace under IFR. Which of the following statements is correct?

A Certain minimum scales of equipment in terms of aircraft instrumentation and radio equipment will apply, as detailed in the Air Navigation Order

B It is advisable to file a flight plan, this may be in the form of a abbreviated flight plan passed by radio to the ATC unit controlling the Control Zone

C You may do so without contacting the relevant ATC unit provided you are flying on the correct quadrantal

D For an IMC rated pilot, IFR flight in Class D airspace is prohibited.

23 You are attempting to maintain a track of 309° (M) whilst tracking away from an NDB. The RBI indicates that you are currently on a track of 314° (M), the aircraft's heading is 309° (M) and the w/v is 270/10. Which of the following statements is correct:

A The aircraft is left of track and must turn right to regain the correct track

B The aircraft is right of track and must turn left to regain the correct track

C The aircraft is right of track, but can maintain heading as the wind will drift the aircraft back onto the correct track

D The aircraft is left of track, but can maintain heading as the wind will drift the aircraft back onto the correct track.

24 Flight into conditions conducive to airframe icing may lead to the aircraft becoming overloaded. If the build up of ice also takes the aircraft centre of gravity forward of the forward limit the most likely consequences are:

A An increased stall speed and a decrease in longitudinal stability

B A decreased stall speed and a decrease in longitudinal stability

C An increased stall speed and an increase in longitudinal stability

D A decreased stall speed and an increase in longitudinal stability.

Questions and Answers
PAPER 3 *for the IMC Rating*

25 Study the runway 27 ILS/DME approach at East Midlands and select the response that correctly matches the information on the chart:

A The ILS frequency is 109.35, coding EME, Sector Safe Altitude when approaching from the north-west is 2700ft

B The procedure turn is flown not below 2000ft QNH, 1720ft QFE, commencing at 6nm DME

C The ILS frequency is 119.65, the procedure commences at 3000ft amsl, the LOM is 4.3nm DME from the runway threshold

D The advisory altitude/height on approach at the L/EME is 2000ft/1720ft, the coding of the L/EME is I EME, the ILS centreline QDM is 272° (M).

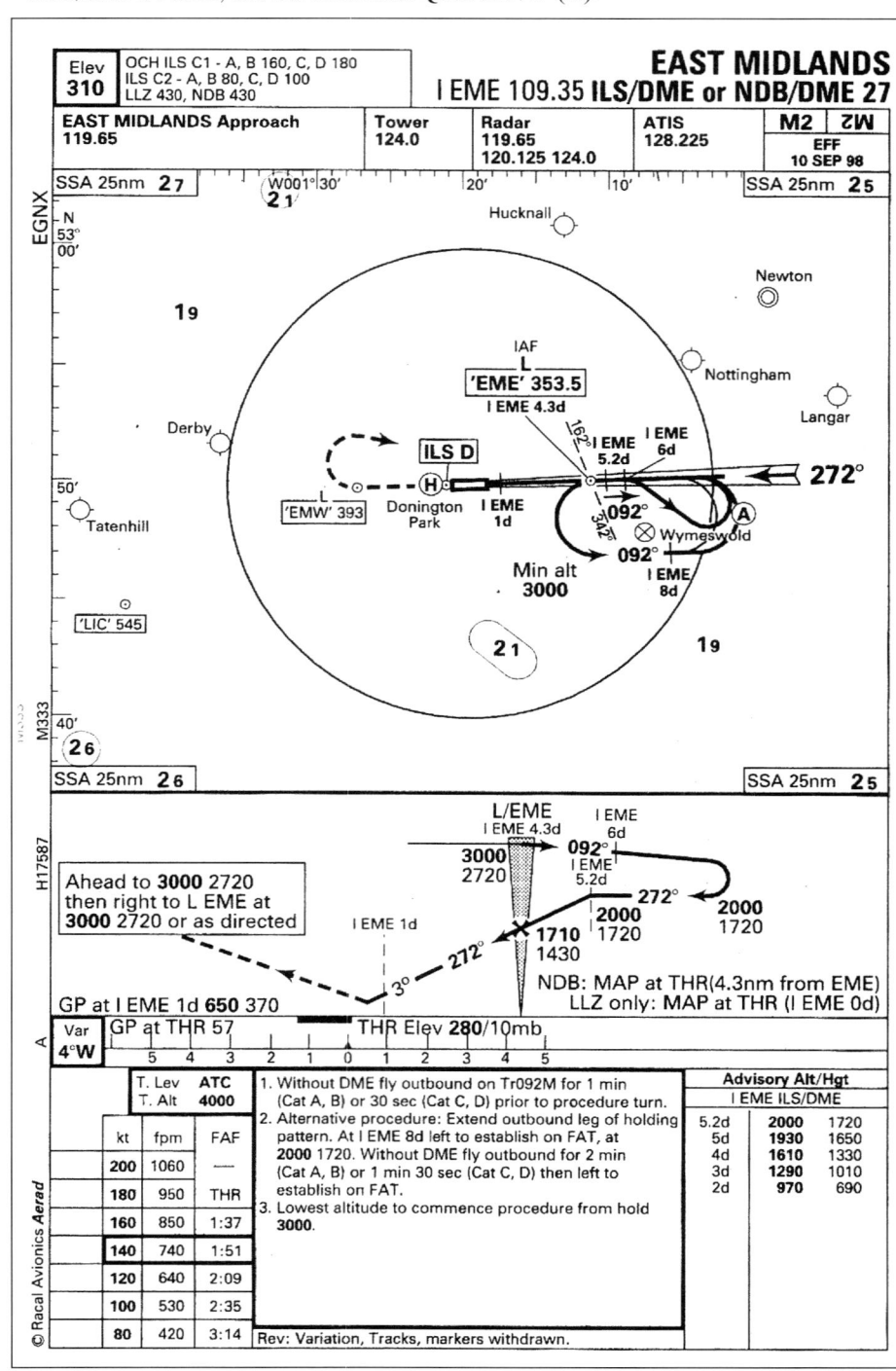

EAST MIDLANDS
I EME 109.35 ILS/DME or NDB/DME 27

Elev 310
OCH ILS C1 - A, B 160, C, D 180
ILS C2 - A, B 80, C, D 100
LLZ 430, NDB 430

| EAST MIDLANDS Approach 119.65 | Tower 124.0 | Radar 119.65 120.125 124.0 | ATIS 128.225 | M2 2W EFF 10 SEP 98 |

SSA 25nm 27 — SSA 25nm 25
EGNX N 53° 00'
W001° 30' 21
Hucknall
Newton
19
IAF L
'EME' 353.5
I EME 4.3d
Nottingham
Langar
Derby
ILS D
I EME 5.2d
I EME 6d
272°
50'
Tatenhill
'EMW' 393
Donington Park
I EME 1d
092°
Wymeswold
Min alt 3000
092°
I EME 8d
'LIC' 545
21 19
40' 26
SSA 25nm 26 — SSA 25nm 25

L/EME I EME 4.3d I EME 6d
3000 2720
092°
I EME 5.2d
272°
2000 1720
2000 1720
Ahead to 3000 2720 then right to L EME at 3000 2720 or as directed
I EME 1d
3° 272°
1710 1720
1430

NDB: MAP at THR(4.3nm from EME)
LLZ only: MAP at THR (I EME 0d)

GP at I EME 1d 650 370
GP at THR 57
THR Elev 280/10mb
Var 4°W

	T. Lev ATC T. Alt 4000	1. Without DME fly outbound on Tr092M for 1 min (Cat A, B) or 30 sec (Cat C, D) prior to procedure turn.	Advisory Alt/Hgt I EME ILS/DME	
kt	fpm	FAF	2. Alternative procedure: Extend outbound leg of holding pattern. At I EME 8d left to establish on FAT, at 2000 1720. Without DME fly outbound for 2 min (Cat A, B) or 1 min 30 sec (Cat C, D) then left to establish on FAT.	5.2d 2000 1720
200	1060	—		5d 1930 1650
180	950	THR		4d 1610 1330
160	850	1:37		3d 1290 1010
140	740	1:51	3. Lowest altitude to commence procedure from hold 3000.	2d 970 690
120	640	2:09		
100	530	2:35		
80	420	3:14	Rev: Variation, Tracks, markers withdrawn.	

Questions and Answers for the IMC Rating PAPER 3

FLIGHT PLAN

Latitude and longitude are given as an aid to identification, but where locations and facilities are marked on the chart, their charted positions should be used.

From	To	Safety Alt ft amsl	FL/Alt	TAS kt	TRk T	W/V	Hdg T	Varn	Hdg M	GS kt	Dist nm	Time min	ETA
HAVERFORDWEST (514959N 0045740W)	BRECON (BCN) (514332N 0031547W)	3400	FL55	110	030/T	030/15		6°W					
BCN	GLOUCESTER (GST) (515331N 0021004W)	3300	FL50	110	030/T	030/15		5°W					
(GST)	DAVENTRY (DTY) (5210049N 001650W)	2400	FL50	110		030/15		5°W					
DTY	MELTON MOWBRAY (524400N 0005324W)	2500	FL50	110		010/15		5°W					
MELTON MOWBRAY (Disused A/D)	GAMSTON (GAM) (531653N 0005650W)	2500	FL50	110		010/15		5°W					
GAM	NETHERTHORPE (531900N 0011148N)	1900	Descent as required	110		005/17		5°W					
ALTERNATE										Totals			
NETHERTHORPE	EAST MIDLANDS (524951N 0011935W)		Descent as required	110		005/17		5°W					

Note: Safety Altitude is derived from the higher of:

(i) the highest ground plus 1299 feet; or
(ii) the highest structure plus 1000 feet; rounded up to the next 100 feet, within 5nm of track.

Questions and Answers
PAPER 3 *for the I M C Rating*

Reference Section
ANSWER PAPER 3

FLIGHT PLAN

Latitude and longitude are given as an aid to identification, but where locations and facilities are marked on the chart, their charted positions should be used.

From	To	Safety Alt ft amsl	FL/Alt	TAS kt	TRk T	W/V	Hdg T	Var	Hdg M	GS kt	Dist nm	Time min	ETA
HAVERFORDWEST (514959N 0045740W)	BRECON (BCN) (514332N 0031547W)	3400	FL55	110	096	030/15	089	6°W	095	102	63	37	
BCN	GLOUCESTER (GST) (515331N 0021004W)	3300	FL50	110	076	030/15	070	5°W	075	99	42	25·5	
(GST)	DAVENTRY (DTY) (521049N 0016505W)	2400	FL50	110	066	030/15	061	5°W	066	97	42·5	26	
DTY	MELTON MOWBRAY (524400N 000524W)	2500	FL50	110	014	010/15	013	5°W	018	95	34	21·5	
MELTON MOWBRAY (Disused A/D)	GAMSTON (GAM) (531653N 0005650W)	2500	FL50	110	356	010/15	358	5°W	003	95	32·5	20·5	
GAM	NETHERTHORPE (531900N 0011148N)	1900	Descent as required	110	284	005/17	293	5°W	298	106	9	5	
									Totals		223	135·5	
ALTERNATE													
NETHERTHORPE	EAST MIDLANDS (524951N 0011935W)	2000	Descent as required	110	189	005/17	190	5°W	195	127	29	13·5	

Note: Safety Altitude is derived from the higher of:
(i) the highest ground plus 1299 feet; or
(ii) the highest structure plus 1000 feet; rounded up to the next 100 feet, within 5nm of track.

Instrument Meteorlogical Conditions

ANSWER PAPER 3

1 B

CAP 53 Part 2 refers. The rating is only valid in UK territorial airspace, in the Channel Islands and Isle of Man airspace.

2 B

Absolute minimum visibility for take-off and landing 1800m.
Minimum visibility for SVFR flight 3km.

Further reference CAP 53.

3 B

The UK Rules of the Air. Rule 29 and 30 apply.

Difference between QNH and Standard pressure is 28mb. This equates (at 1mb/30 ft) to 840ft. As QNH is low, altimeter will read high when set to 1013mb, therefore FL40 equates to 3160ft QNH. As the terrain is 3200ft amsl, and there may be an unmarked obstacle up to 299ft agl, 3160ft is clearly too low. FL60 would be required to obey the IFR.

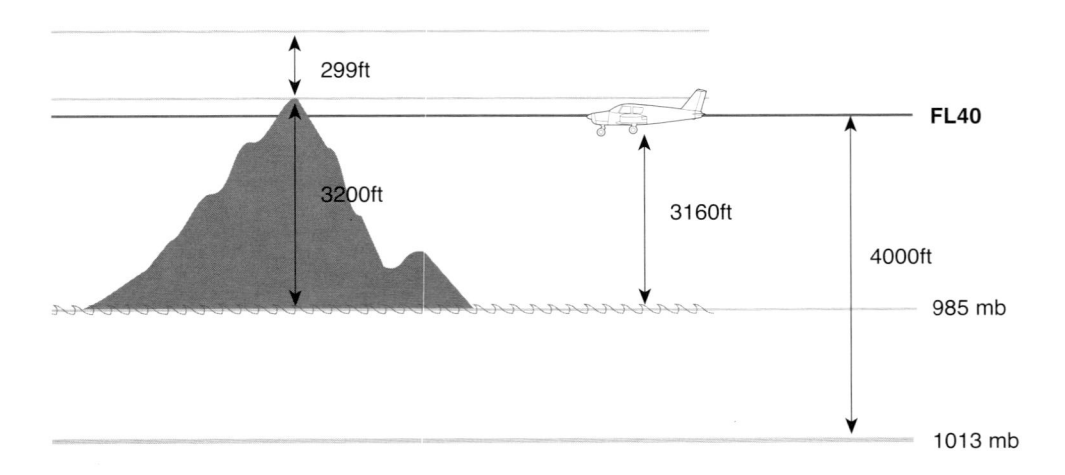

Further reference: The Private Pilot's Licence Course Book 2 (Air Law and Radiotelephony), Visual Flight Rules / Instrument Flight Rules section; and The Private Pilot's Licence Course Book 3 (Navigation, Meteorolgy and Flight Planning) Vertical Navigation section.

4 C

From 1600 hrs the cloudbase is forecast to lower to 300ft. The absolute minimum MDH for an IMC rated pilot on a non-precision approach such an NDB/DME approach is 600ft. The actual MDH for this individual case may be higher. Thus plan to arrive before 1600 hrs when the cloudbase is forecast to be 1200ft.

Further reference on decoding weather reports in The Private Pilot's Licence Course Book 3 (Navigation, Meteorolgy and Flight Planning), Aviation Weather Reports and forecasts section.

5 C

Relying on seat of the pants information without adequate visual references will quickly lead to spatial disorientation. Therefore when flying in the situation described it is vital to use the flight instruments.

Further reference: The Private Pilot's Licence Course Book 1 (Flying Training), Exercise 19, Instrument Flying.

Reference Section

ANSWER PAPER 3

6 A

From the competed flight plan the track (T) should be 096°.
Apply the magnetic variation for the area of 6°W (remembering to add westerly variation) so track (M) = 102°

Further reference: The Private Pilot's Licence Course Book 3 (Navigation, Meteorolgy and Flight Planning), Aeronautical Maps section.

7 B

From the competed flight plan heading (T) should be 061° (T). As a gross error check note that the wind is from the left of track, so the aircraft has to head slightly into wind to maintain track. Remember to apply the magnetic variation (5°W), thus 061° + 5° = HDG (M) 066°

Further reference: The Private Pilot's Licence Course Book 3 (Navigation, Meteorology and Flight Planning), Navigation Principles 1 section.

8 D

From the completed flight plan form. On the 1:500,000 Southern England chart the highest terrain within 5nm of the track between Netherthorpe and East Midlands is the spot height of 659ft amsl west of Mansfield. 659ft is rounded up to 700ft, + 299ft for an unmarked obstacle = 999ft (say 1000ft). Adding the 1000ft safety margin gives 2000ft.

Note that the highest point en-route are the masts at 759ft just south of Long Eaton. However, rounding these up to 800ft and adding 1000ft = 1800ft.

As this is lower than the 2000ft figure calculated on the basis of the highest terrain, it is disregarded in favour of the higher figure. See the notes on Safety Altitude calculation under the flight plan form.

Further reference: The Private Pilot's Licence Course Book 3 (Navigation, Meteorology and Flight Planning), Vertical Navigation section.

9 B

Taken from the competed flight plan. As a gross error check, note that the aircraft is heading into wind, and so groundspeed can be expected to be less than TAS.

Further reference: The Private Pilot's Licence Course Book 3 (Navigation, Meteorology and Flight Planning), Navigation Principles 2 section.

10 C

From the competed flight plan add up the leg distances, the total should come to 223nm. Note the use of different units in the possible answers.

Further reference: The Private Pilot's Licence Course Book 3 (Navigation, Meteorolgy and Flight Planning), Aeronautical Maps section.

11 C

Add up the remaining leg times from Daventry to Netherthorpe, they should come to 47 minutes – remember you are already at Daventry! 0945 + 47 minutes = ETA 1032.

Further reference: The Private Pilot's Licence Course Book 3 (Navigation, Meteorolgy and Flight Planning), Aeronautical Maps section.

Instrument Meteorological Conditions

ANSWER PAPER 3

12 C

Calculate fuel required using the flight computer set to 65 lb/hr:

Haverfordwest to Netherthorpe 135·5 mins @ 65 lb/hr = 147lbs
Netherthorpe to East Midlands 13·5 mins @ 65 lb/hr = 15lbs
Hold   45 mins @ 65 lb/hr = 49lbs.

Complete the table by adding all quantities:

15 + 147 + 22 + 15 + 15 + 49 + 65 = 328lbs.

To convert weight to volume at a Specific Gravity (SG) of ·72, set up the flight computer as shown to obtain as answer of 45 imp gal (to nearest imperial gallon).

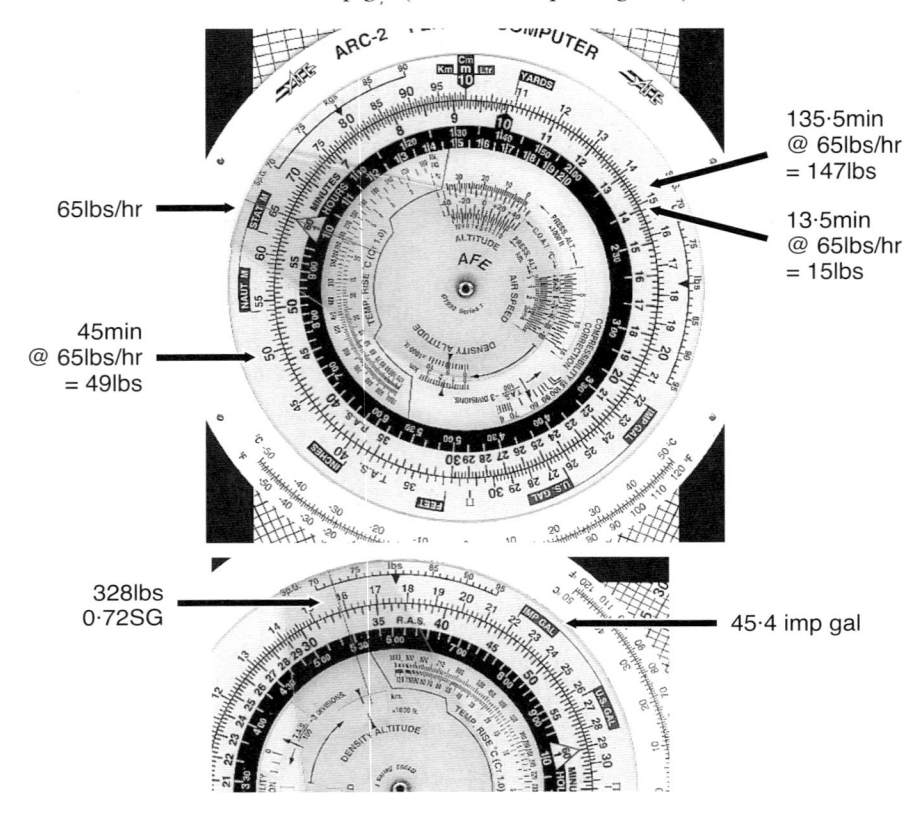

- 65lbs/hr
- 135·5min @ 65lbs/hr = 147lbs
- 13·5min @ 65lbs/hr = 15lbs
- 45min @ 65lbs/hr = 49lbs
- 328lbs 0·72SG
- 45·4 imp gal

Further reference: The Private Pilot's Licence Course Book 3 (Navigation, Meteorolgy and Flight Planning), Fuel Planning and Performance sections.

13 C

Refer to UK AIP ENR 1.6 and the ICAO 1:500,000 Southern England chart.
This area is covered by Brize Norton LARS on 134.300.

Reference Section

ANSWER PAPER 3

14 D

Using the flight computer
50 US gal at SG .72 =   300lbs.

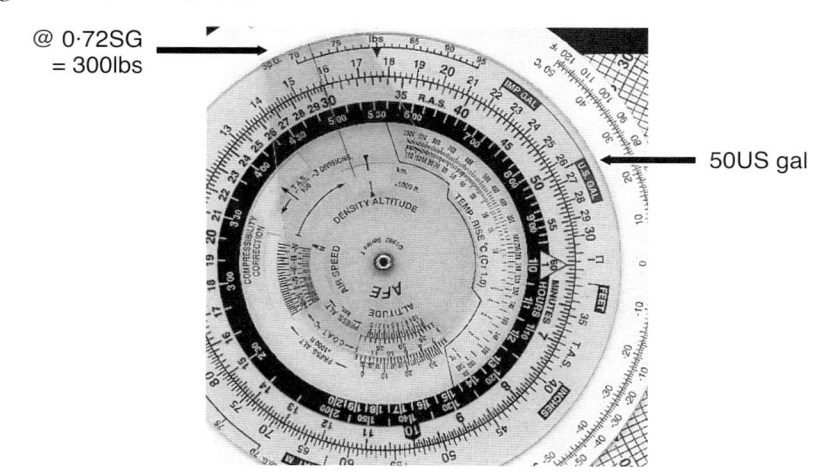

@ 0·72SG
= 300lbs

50US gal

Basic aircraft weight	=	1525lbs
Fuel	=	300lbs
Pilot	=	185lbs
Pass	=	350lbs
Baggage	=	40lbs
TOTAL		2400lbs

The Maximum Landing Weight is 2300lbs. Therefore 100lbs of fuel must be burnt off before landing.

Using the flight computer, 100lbs at SG .72 = 17 US gal (to the nearest gallon).

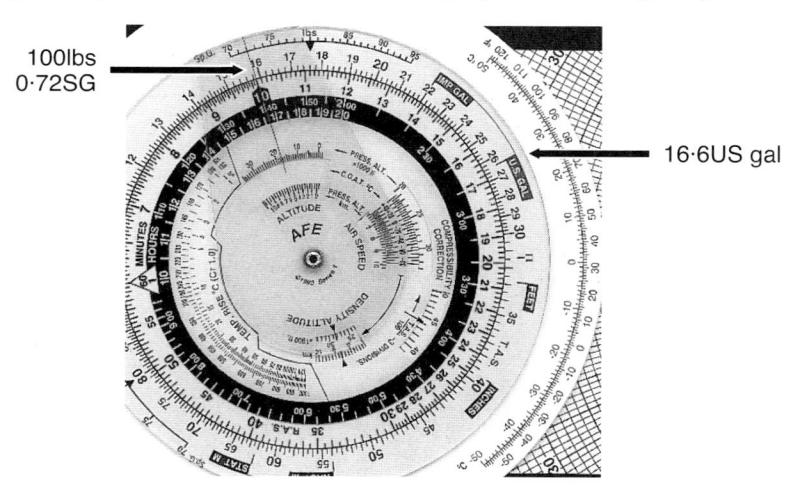

100lbs
0·72SG

16·6US gal

Further reference: The Private Pilot's Licence Course Book 3 (Navigation, Meteorolgy and Flight Planning), Performance section.

15 C

UK AIP GEN 3 refers.

NDB range is based on a daytime protection ratio between wanted and unwanted signals, that limits bearing errors at that distance to ± 5° or less.

Instrument Meteorlogical Conditions

ANSWER PAPER 3

16 D

The diagram shows each of the possible answers, and their correct quadrantal positions in relation to the VOR. Sketching a diagram such as this for yourself avoids much in the way of mental gymnastics in answering a question like this one!

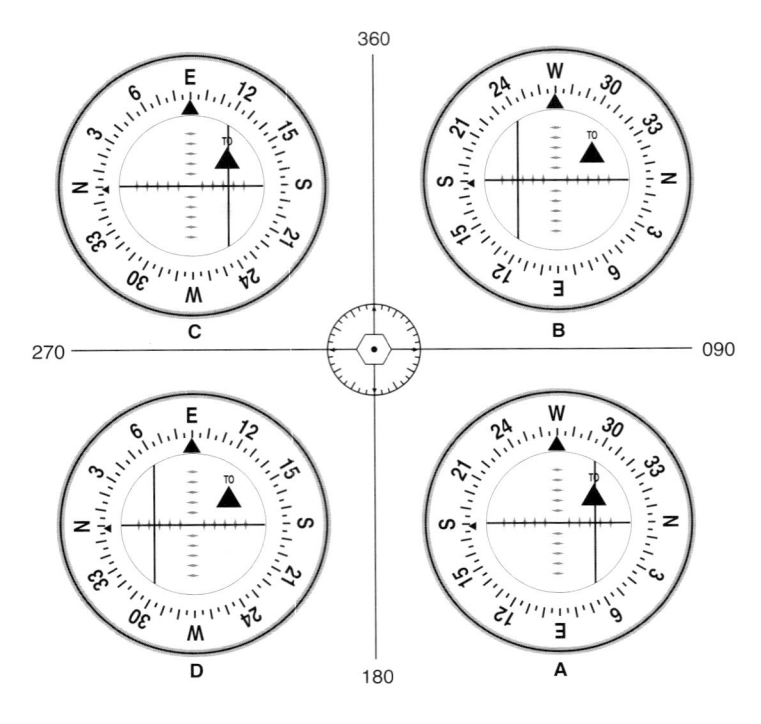

17 A

This is a **VFR** clearance, not a SVFR clearance, so the pilot is not absolved from any of the Rule 5 provisions.

Further reference: The Private Pilot's Licence Course Book 2 (Air Law and Radiotelephony), Visual Flight Rules / Instrument Flight Rules and Rules of the Air and Air Traffic Control sections.

18 D

The diagram below shows the localiser coverage of a UK ILS. There is usually a pink AIC current, regarding the use of ILSs in the UK.

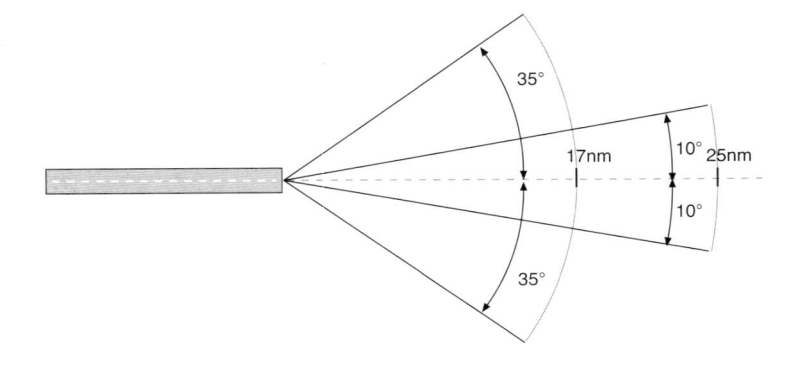

19 D

A terminal DME as used in association with an ILS will have its reply pulse modified to display to the pilot range from threshold of the runway to which the ILS is selected, rather than slant range from the beacon.

20 D

UK AIP AD 1.1.2. Calculation of approach minima refers.
System minimum 300ft
OCH   350ft
AS OCH is higher than system minimum use this figure as a basis for MDH calculation.
So, OCH   350ft
IMC allowance 200ft
               550ft
Recommended absolute minimum for IMC rated pilots is 600ft, so as this figure is higher than OCH + 200, 600ft is your MDH for this approach.

21 A

The basic flight instrument checks when taxying:

Attitude Indicator -   Erect, no pitch or bank indications
Turn Co-ordinator-   Needle left, ball right and vice versa
HI & Compass   -   Decreasing headings when turning left, increasing when turning right.

Further reference: The Private Pilot's Licence Course Book 1 (Flying Training), Exercise 5, Taxying.

22 A

UK Rules of the Air refer.

Note, it is MANDATORY to file a full flight plan for an IFR flight in controlled airspace, this requirement is not satisfied by passing an abbreviated flight plan to the relevant ATC unit (this only suffices for a VFR flight).

Further reference: The Private Pilot's Licence Course Book 2 (Air Law and Radiotelephony), Visual Flight Rules / Instrument Flight Rules and Aeronauticl Information Service sections. The Private Pilot's Licence Course Book 3 (Navigation, Meteorolgy and Flight Planning), The Full Flight Plan.

23 B

As seen from the diagram, to regain track a left turn is required. Note that the wind will attempt to drift the aircraft further off-track.

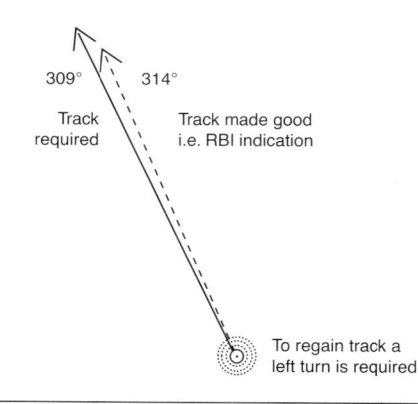

309° Track required
314° Track made good i.e. RBI indication
To regain track a left turn is required

24 C

An overloaded aeroplane will stall at a higher IAS than an aeroplane that is not overweight. With the Centre of Gravity forward the tailplane has a long moment arm and the aeroplane will be very stable in the pitching plane, the forward C of G also increases the stall airspeed.

25 B

Instrument Meteorlogical Conditions
ANSWER PAPER 3

Questions and Answers for the IMC Rating **PAPER 4**

Instructions

1. Time allowed 2 hours.

2. Twenty five multi-choice questions each carrying 4 marks. Marks are not deducted for wrong answers. The pass mark is 72% (i.e. 18 questions or more must be answered correctly).

3. Unless otherwise specified, the questions relate to a UK licenced pilot, operating a UK registered aircraft in UK airspace.

4. Read each question carefully as there is only one answer which is correct.

5. Remember examination technique, you are advised to pass over questions that seem difficult at first sight and return to them when you have answered the others.

Questions and Answers
for the IMC Rating PAPER 4

1 Which of the following statements indicates part of the revalidation requirement for the IMC rating?

A To fly an instrument approach every 28 days

B To fly at least 5 hours in IMC every 13 months

C To show log book evidence of flying an instrument approach that is different from that flown on the previous test whilst accompanied by a flying instructor qualified to give instrument flying instruction

D To fly 5 instrument approaches every 13 months.

2 One of the privileges of the IMC rating is:

A To allow flight in IMC in Class D airspace

B To allow the pilot to cross an airway

C To allow the pilot to take-off or land when the visibility is less than 1800m

D To allow flight out of sight of the surface when in receipt of a Special VFR clearance.

3 Whilst cruising outside controlled airspace you encounter IMC and elect to climb to a suitable Quadrantal cruising level. Given the regional QNH is 995mb, your track is 268° (T) (variation 4°W) and the highest obstacle within 5nm of track is 3350ft amsl, the appropriate Flight Level should be:

A FL65

B FL60

C FL45

D FL40.

4 A METAR obtained for your destination reads:
231720Z 18004KT 2000 HZ 05/04 Q1033
It is your intention to arrive at destination 30 minutes after sunset. You should be aware that:

A Visibility will remain above IMC rating limits

B Visibility will remain below IMC rating limits

C There is a risk of fog forming after sunset as temperature decreases and you should be prepared to divert

D The METAR shows a risk of rain ice conditions.

5 When rolling out of a rate 1 turn which has taken 1 minute to complete your vestibular apparatus will:

A React in agreement with the aircraft instruments

B Give the sensation of a turn that is opposite to that which has been occurring, even though that turn has just ceased

C Give the sensation of a turn that is the same as that which has been occurring, even though that turn has just ceased

D Give the sensation of rolling and pitching up as the turn is completed.

Questions and Answers
PAPER 4 *for the IMC Rating*

Complete the attached flight plan using an ICAO 1:500,000 chart for Southern England or Northern England then answer questions 6-13

6 What is the Safety Altitude between MONA and W00330?

A 4800ft

B 4600ft

C 3900ft

D 3800ft.

7 What is the Magnetic track between W00330 and WREXHAM?

A 096°

B 103°

C 108°

D 113°.

8 What is the groundspeed between TRENT and GAMSTON?

A 130kt

B 125kt

C 120kt

D 115kt.

9 What is the Magnetic heading betweeen GAMSTON and STURGATE?

A 052°

B 057°

C 062°

D 067°.

10 What would be the lowest appropriate Quadrantal Cruising Level between MONA and W00330 (assume 1mb = 30ft)?

A FL45

B FL50

C FL55

D FL60.

11 What is the total elapsed time for the flight from MONA to STURGATE (to the nearest minute)?

A 1hr 9mins

B 1hr 16mins

C 50mins

D 54mins.

12 Find the minimum fuel uplift required for this flight (to the nearest US gal) given:

Start, Taxy and Take-off and climb	3US gal
Mona to Sturgate @ 9US gal/hr	
Approach and Missed Approach	4US gal
Divert Sturgate to Waddington @ 9US gal/hr	
Approach and Landing	3US gal
Hold 45mins @ 9US gal/hr	
Reserve	9US gal

A 35US gal

B 38US gal

C 43US gal

D 46US gal.

---

13 Which is the most appropriate Air Traffic Control Unit to contact for a Radar Information Service to cover the area between MANSFIELD and STURGATE:

A Waddington 127.35

B Conningsby 120.80

C Scampton 127.35

D Cranwell 119.37.

---

14 Whilst in receipt of a Radar Information Service (RIS) from Aerodrome A you wish to penetrate the Aerodrome Traffic Zone at Aerodrome B. Responsibility for obtaining clearance into the ATZ lies with:

A Aerodrome A, being the provider of the RIS

B The Flight Information Service

C The Lower Airspace Radar Service

D The pilot.

Questions and Answers
PAPER 4 *for the I M C Rating*

Refer to the UK AIP extract below, then answer Q15.

| Whitegate NDB | WHI | 368·5kHz | H24 | 531106N 0023723W | – | Range 25nm. |

15 Whilst tracking between WREXHAM and TRENT you intend to use the WHITEGATE NDB for cross cuts. Up to what range from WHITEGATE can you receive a reliable signal?

A 40nm

B 25nm

C 15nm

D 10nm.

16 A VOR indicator is observed to show a 4 dot CDI deflection to the left. If the OBS is set to read 224° FROM, the aircraft is actually on:

A The 216° radial

B The 232° radial

C The 036° radial

D The 056° radial.

17 Having tuned a VOR and set the OBS to 270° you note that the 'TO' flag is visible and the CDI shows fly left. These indications suggest that you are located relative to the VOR in the sector defined by:

A 270° - 359°

B 180° - 269°

C 090° - 179°

D 360° - 089°.

18 Deflection of the Localiser and glidepath needles of an ILS display will indicate a deviation from localiser and Gide Path centre lines of:

	Localiser	Glide Path
A	2°/dot	0.14°/dot
B	0.14°/dot	½°/dot
C	½°/dot	0.14°/dot
D	½°/dot	½°/dot.

19 In the Northern Hemisphere, when turning right through a southerly heading the compass:

A Will be 'sluggish' and show a heading less than the actual

B Will show the actual heading consistently

C Will be 'lively' and show a heading greater than the actual

D Will be in error by the amount indicated on the correction card.

20 An IMC rated pilot flying a single engine aircraft on a private flight should be aware that for take-off the recommended minima are:

A A cloudbase of at least 600ft and an RVR of at least 1800m

B A cloudbase of at least 600ft and an RVR of at least 1000m

C A cloudbase of at least 200ft and an RVR of at least 1800m

D A cloudbase that will allow successful completion of the published IAP should an immediate return after take-off be required.

21 During the climb it is discovered that the static vents have become blocked. Which of the following options best describes the effect on the altimeter and ASI as the climb continues?

	Altimeter	**ASI**
A	Underread	Underread
B	Overread	Underread
C	Underread	Overread
D	Overread	Overread.

22 Having obtained a Special VFR clearance into a Control Zone (CTR) to land at an airfield within the CTR, your aircraft suffers a radio failure. If you have entered the CTR the correct course of action would be to:

A Leave the CTR by the shortest route and land at a suitable airfield outside controlled airspace

B Proceed to the aerodrome in accordance with the SVFR clearance and land as soon as possible

C Proceed to the aerodrome in accordance with the SVFR clearance whilst flying a left handed triangular pattern every 3 minutes

D Leave the CTR whilst selecting Code 7700 on the transponder.

23 An aircraft with a MAUW of 1050kg has been loaded to a mass of 1200kg. Compared to an aircraft which is properly loaded which of the following statements is true?

A The overloaded aircraft will require a longer take-off run, but overall take-off distance will be unchanged

B The overloaded aircraft will have a slower stalling speed

C The overloaded aircraft will have a faster lift-off speed and require a longer take-off distance

D The overloaded aircraft will not get off the ground.

Questions and Answers
PAPER 4 *for the I M C Rating*

24 Given the data below what would be the combined maximum weight of passengers and baggage that could be loaded without overloading the aircraft?

Aircraft Basic Weight	1405lbs
Maximum Take-Off Weight	2400lbs
Pilot	190lbs
Fuel - 40imp gal (S.G. ·72)	

A 674lbs

B 604lbs

C 564lbs

D 517lbs.

25 With reference to the Metform 215 below, which of the following statements best reflects the effect of the forecast weather on the flight from MONA to STURGATE with a planned departure time of 0900Z:

A There will be no adverse effects. The weather is within the limits specified for an IMC rated pilot

B The freezing level of 1000ft would preclude flight in most light aircraft

C It is likely that the weather at Mona may be below limits for take-off from time to time. Be prepared to delay departure until conditions indicated by the outlook move in

D Zone 3 conditions will preclude safe flight on the route.

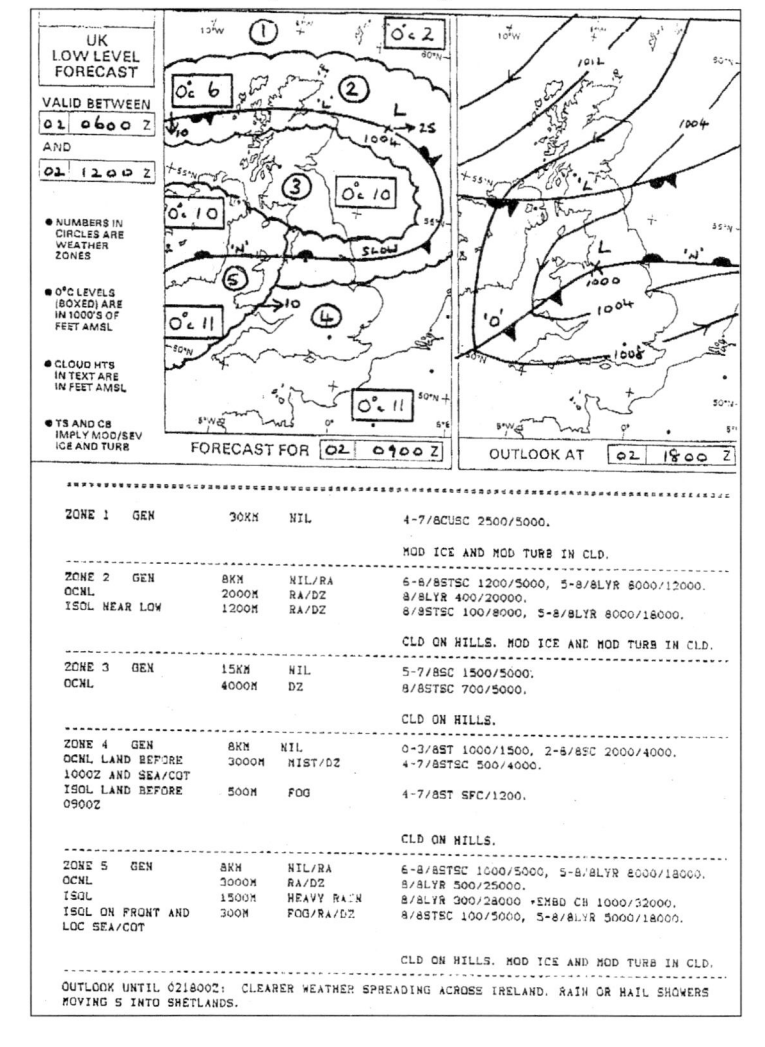

Questions and Answers for the IMC Rating — PAPER 4

FLIGHT PLAN

Latitude and longitude are given as an aid to identification, but where locations and facilities are marked on the chart, their charted positions should be used.

From	To	Safety Alt ft amsl	FL/Alt	TAS kt	Trk T	W/V	Hdg T	Varn	Hdg M	GS kt	Dist nm	Time min	ETA
MONA (531532N 0042223W)	TOP OF CLIMB		↗			190/10		6°W			11·5		
TOP OF CLIMB	0033000W TOP OF CLIMB		FL55	100		190/10		6°W			20·5 / 32		
W00330	WREXHAM Disused A/D (530354N 0025700W)		FL55	120		200/10		6°W					
WREXHAM	TRENT (TNT) (530314N 0014012W)	3200	FL55 ↘	120		190/10		5°W					
TNT	GAMSTON (GAM) (531653N 0005650W)	2600	2800	120		180/12		5°W					
GAM	STURGATE (532252N 0004107W)	2600	2800	120		180/12		5°W					
ALTERNATE		1800	Descent as required	120		180/12		5°W		Totals			
STURGATE	GAMSTON (GAM) (531653N 0005650W)	1800	Descent as required	120		190/12		5°W					
GAM	WADDINGTON (530957N W0003126W)	1800	Descent as required	120		190/12		5°W					

Note: Safety Altitude is derived from the higher of:
(i) the highest ground plus 1299 feet; or
(ii) the highest structure plus 1000 feet;
rounded up to the next 100 feet, within 5nm of track.

Instrument Meteorlogical Conditions
ANSWER PAPER 4

Reference Section
ANSWER PAPER 4

FLIGHT PLAN

Latitude and longitude are given as an aid to identification, but where locations and facilities are marked on the chart, their charted positions should be used.

From	To	Safety Alt ft amsl	FL/Alt	TAS kt	Trk T	W/V	Hdg T	Varn	Hdg M	GS kt	Dist nm	Time min	ETA
MONA (531532N 0042223W)	TOP OF CLIMB	4800	FL55 ↗	100	102	190/10	108	6°W	114	99	11·5 / 32	7	
TOP OF CLIMB	003000W	4800	FL55	120	102	190/10	108	6°W	114	99	20·5		
W00330	WREXHAM Disused A/D (530354N 0025700W)	3200	FL55	120	102	200/10	107	6°W	113	121	20	10	
WREXHAM	TRENT (TNT) (530314N 0014012W)	2600	FL55 ↘	120	091	180/12	097	5°W	102	119	46	23	
TNT	GAMSTON (GAM) (531653N 0005650W)	2600	2800	120	062	180/12	067	5°W	072	125	30	14	
GAM	STURGATE (532252.N 0004107W)	1800	Descent as required	120	057	180/12	062	5°W	067	126	10·5	5	
									Totals		138.5	69	
ALTERNATE													
STURGATE	GAMSTON (GAM) (531653N 0005650W)	1800	Descent as required	120	237	190/12	232	5°W	237	113	10·5	5·5	
GAM	WADDINGTON (530957N 0003126W)	1800	Descent as required	120	114	190/12	119	5°W	124	115	16·5	8·5	

Note: Safety Altitude is derived from the higher of:
(i) the highest ground plus 1299 feet; or
(ii) the highest structure plus 1000 feet;
rounded up to the next 100 feet, within 5nm of track.

Instrument Meteorlogical Conditions

ANSWER PAPER 4

1 C

CAP 53 Section 2 refers. This must be done before the revalidation flight test. As an alternative you can opt to do two different types of approach during the flight test, although not many people take this option!

2 A

CAP 53, Section 2 refers.

3 A

The UK Rules of the Air. Rules 29 and Rule 30 apply.

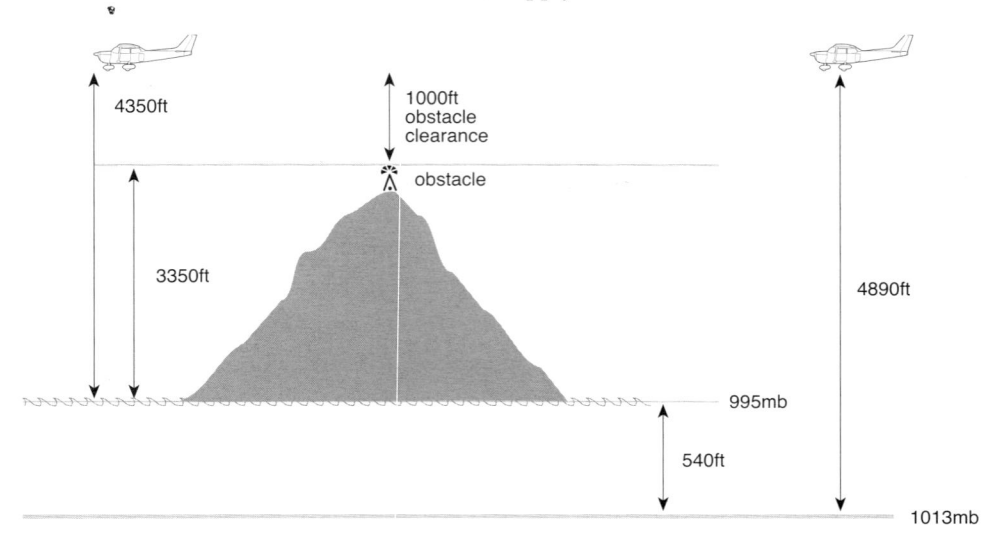

[Diagram showing an aircraft at 4350ft on the left, a mountain with an obstacle on top, 1000ft obstacle clearance above the obstacle, 3350ft from sea level to obstacle top, and on the right an aircraft at 4890ft above 1013mb datum, with 540ft between 995mb (sea level) and 1013mb datum.]

The difference between QNH and Standard pressure is 18mb. This equates (at 1mb/30ft) to 540ft.

As QNH is low (less than 1013mb), the altimeter will read high when set to 1013.

So, obstacle + 1000ft equates to 4890ft with altimeter set to 1013.

Next determine the track (M).

Track (T) 268° + var 4°W (West is Best) = track (M) 272°

Thus a Flight Level of EVEN + 500 ft is required.

The lowest useable flight level is FL65. Use of FL45 would compromise the IFR obstacle clearance requirement.

Further reference: The Private Pilot's Licence Course Book 2 (Air Law and Radiotelephony), Visual Flight Rules / Instrument Flight Rules section; and The Private Pilot's Licence Course Book 3 (Navigation, Meteorology and Flight Planning) Vertical Navigation section.

4 C

The METAR shows high pressure, high humidity, no cloud and poor visibility. These are all good indicators for the possible formation of fog after sunset as the temperature drops.

Further reference: The Private Pilot's Licence Course Book 3 (Navigation, Meteorolgy and Flight Planning) Visibility and Aviation Weather Reports and Forecasts section.

5 B

This is a case of vestibular illusion caused by roll. Since the resultant of the weight and turning force vectors is aligned with the pilot's head-foot axis in a co-ordinated turn, the pilot may perceive his orientation as wings level. In this case, when rolling out of a turn to a wings level attitude, the pilot may feel as though (s)he has actually banked away from wings level. This illusion is commonly known as the leans.

6 A

From the completed flight plan. On the 1:500,000 chart the highest obstacle within 5nm of the track between MONA and W00330 is the spot height of 3491ft amsl. Add to this the allowance for unmarked obstacles of 299ft and the IFR obstacle clearance allowance of 1000ft. Now round up to the next hundred.
Thus MSA is 4800ft.

Further reference: The Private Pilot's Licence Course Book 3 (Navigation, Meteorology and Flight Planning), Vertical Navigation section.

7 C

From the completed flight plan track (T) is 102°
Apply the magnetic variation for the area 6°W (Remember 'West is best' so add):

$102° + 6° = 108°$ (M)

Further reference: The Private Pilot's Licence Course Book 3 (Navigation, Meteorology and Flight Planning), Aeronautical Maps section.

8 B

Taken from the completed flight plan. As a gross error check note that angle between wind and track gives a tailwind.

Further reference: The Private Pilot's Licence Course Book 3 (Navigation, Meteorology and Flight Planning), Navigation Principles 2 section.

9 D

Taken from the completed flight plan.

Track (T) is 057°. Applying correction for wind using the computer should give 062°. As a gross error check the wind is from the right, so the aircraft has turned right slightly to maintain track. Apply the magnetic variation for the area of 5°W, $062° + 5° = 067°$

Further reference: The Private Pilot's Licence Course Book 3 (Navigation, Meteorology and Flight Planning), Navigation Principles 1 section.

10 C

MONA - W00330, track (T) 102° + Var 6°W = track (M) 108°

In this quadrant ODD + 500 FLs apply, the first above the safety altitude is FL55.
(Note: this question assumes that the QNH is close to Standard Pressure i.e. 1013mb).
For the purposes of the exam you should assume this unless the question states otherwise.

Further reference: The Private Pilot's Licence Course Book 2 (Air Law and Radiotelephony), Visual Flight Rules / Instrument Flight Rules section; and The Private Pilot's Licence Course Book 3 (Navigation, Meteorology and Flight Planning) Vertical Navigation section.

11 A

Add up the leg times on the flight plan, the answer should be 1 hr 9 minutes.

Instrument Meteorlogical Conditions

ANSWER PAPER 4

12 B

Use the flight computer to calculate fuel required as follows:

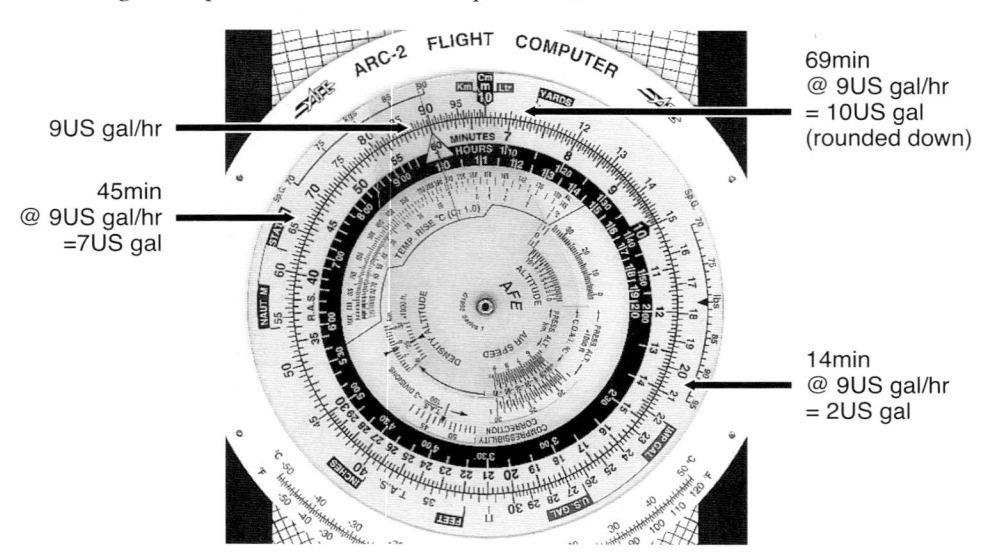

- 9US gal/hr
- 45min @ 9US gal/hr = 7US gal
- 69min @ 9US gal/hr = 10US gal (rounded down)
- 14min @ 9US gal/hr = 2US gal

Mona to Sturgate - 69 minutes @ 9 US gal/hr = 10 US gal
Sturgate to Waddington - 14 minutes @ 9 US gal/hr = 2 US gal
Hold - 45 minutes @ 9US gal/hr = 7 US gal

Complete the table by adding all quantities:

3 + 10 + 4 + 2 + 3 + 7 + 9 = 38 US gal.

Further reference: The Private Pilot's Licence Course Book 3 (Navigation, Meteorology and Flight Planning), Fuel Planning section.

13 A

Refer to the 1:500,000 chart legend and also UK AIP ENR 1.6 Section.

14 D

UK AIP ENR 1.6 Section refers.

Further reference: The Private Pilot's Licence Course Book 2 (Air Law and Radiotelephony), En Route Procedures section.

15 B

Refer to UK AIP ENR extract for WHITEGATE NDB. In the remarks column note the range of the NDB is 25nm.

16 B

Each dot of CDI deflection (when a VOR is selected) is equivalent to 2°. Therefore a 4 dot deflection = 8°. The CDI is giving a 'fly left' indication, so the aircraft is 8° right of the 224° radial, on the 232° radial.

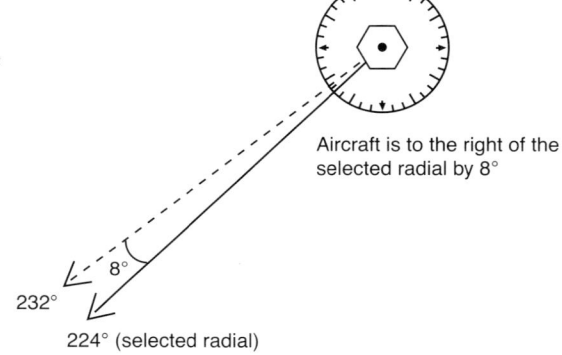

Aircraft is to the right of the selected radial by 8°

232°
224° (selected radial)

Reference Section
ANSWER PAPER 4

17 D

The diagram shows the CDI as it would appear from answer D.

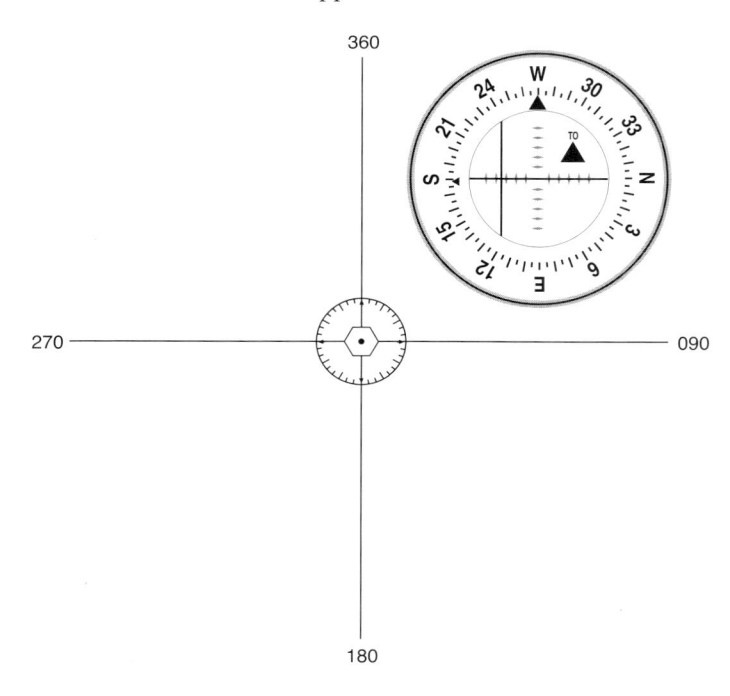

18 C

ILS Localiser deviation scale - 0·5° per dot
ILS Glide Path deviation scale - 0·14° per dot

There is usually a current pink AIC describing the ILS.

19 C

Further reference: The Private Pilot's Licence Course Book 3 (Navigation, Meteorolgy and Flight Planning) Special Navigation Situations section, The Private Pilot's Licence Course Book 1 (Flying Training)
Exercise 9, Turning.

20 A

UK AIP AD 1.1.2 refers.

21 A

The altimeter is connected to the static vent. Without static pressure entering the system the altimeter hands will not move, in effect, as the aeroplane climbs, the altimeter will continue to indicate the altitude at which the blockage occurred. As this is lower than the actual altitude the altimeter is said to be underreading.

The static pressure trapped in the case of the ASI will be at a higher density (and pressure) than the static element of the total pressure detected by the pitot tube. Consequently this imbalance of static pressures will restrict capsule expansion and cause the ASI to underread (showing an airspeed less than actual).

22 B

UK AIP ENR 1.6. Radio failure procedures refer.

Further reference: The Private Pilot's Licence Course Book 2 (Air Law and Radiotelephony), Communications Failure section.

Instrument Meteorlogical Conditions

ANSWER PAPER 4

23 C

The stalling speed of the overloaded aircraft will be faster, so lift-off speed and take-off distance will be increased.

Further reference: The Private Pilot's Licence Course Book 4 Technical; Loading and Performance Section

24 D

Calculate the fuel weight using the flight computer:

40 imp gal @ SG .72 = 288lbs

Basic aircraft	=	1405lbs
Fuel (40 imp gal)	=	288lbs
Pilot	=	190lbs

      SUB TOTAL 1883lbs

Subtract 1883lbs from the maximum weight to give allowable payload (passengers and baggage):

2400 - 1883 = 517lbs.

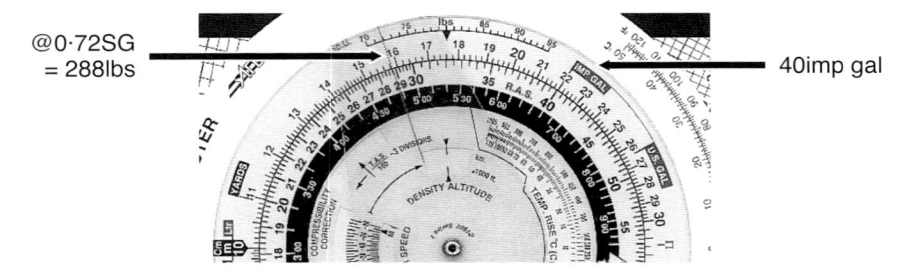

@0·72SG = 288lbs   ⟶   ⟵ 40imp gal

Further reference: The Private Pilot's Licence Course Book 3 (Navigation, Meteorology and Flight Planning), Performance section.

25 C

Refer to the Metform 215. At the departure time, Mona is in Zone 5. Conditions in Zone 5. particularly near the front and near the coast (Mona qualifies on both counts) include poor visibility in rain and drizzle, fog and low cloud, which will put conditions outside the recommended take-off minima (1800m/600ft). Therefore an 0900Z departure looks unlikely. However, the outlook indicates the front 'N' moving south away from Mona, with the probability of clearer weather moving in. By delaying the departure the pilot can assess the conditions as the situation develops. Remember that a new Metform 215 will be issued soon after 0900Z, and as more airfields (including the destination) open more weather reports and forecasts will be available.

Further reference: The Private Pilot's Licence Course Book 3 (Navigation, Meteorology and Flight Planning), Aviation Weather Reports and Forecasts section.

Questions and Answers
for the IMC Rating **PAPER 5**

Instructions

1 Time allowed 2 hours.

2 Twenty five multi-choice questions each carrying 4 marks. Marks are not deducted for wrong answers. The pass mark is 72% (i.e. 18 questions or more must be answered correctly).

3 Unless otherwise specified, the questions relate to a UK licenced pilot, operating a UK registered aircraft in UK airspace.

4 Read each question carefully as there is only one answer which is correct.

5 Remember examination technique, you are advised to pass over questions that seem difficult at first sight and return to them when you have answered the others.

Questions and Answers
for the IMC Rating PAPER 5

1 Which of the following responses best describes the actions necessary to undertake an IFR flight within Class D airspace?

(i) File a full flight plan.

(ii) Obey rule 29 (minimum height) and rule 5 (low flying).

(iii) Contact the appropriate ATC unit, obtaining the necessary clearance, listening out, making position reports and obeying ATC instructions.

(iv) Fly at the correct quadrantal FL.

(v) Be able to maintain a minimum flight visibility of 3km.

A (i) to (v) inclusive

B (ii), (iii) and (iv)

C (ii) to (iv) inclusive

D (i) to (iii) inclusive.

---

2 Revalidation of an IMC rating is achieved by:

A Undertaking a flight test every 25 months

B Obtaining a Certificate of Experience every 25 months

C Undertaking a flight test every 13 months

D Obtaining a Certificate of Experience every 13 months.

---

3 Which of the following best describes the vertical dimensions of a Military Aerodrome Traffic Zone (MATZ)?

A A circular zone extending to 3000ft above aerodrome level (aal), with the 'stub' extending from 1000ft aal to 3000ft aal

B A circular zone extending to 3000ft above mean sea level (amsl), with the 'stub' extending from 1000ft amsl to 3000ft amsl

C A circular zone extending to 3000ft above mean sea level (amsl), with the 'stub' extending from 1000ft aal to 3000ft aal

D A circular zone extending to 3000ft above aerodrome level (aal), with the 'stub' extending from 1000ft aal to 5000ft aal.

---

4 On departure from aerodrome 'X' you are offered the following clearance:

"After take-off turn on track to leave the zone, via the city centre, not above 2000ft QNH, Special VFR".

Assuming that the city centre is a 'congested area' which of the following statements is correct?

A You are not exempt from any of the rule 5 (low flying) provisions by this clearance

B You may fly above 2000ft QNH if necessary in order to respect the rule 5 (low flying) provisions, provided you are carrying a mode 'c' transponder

C You are exempt the '1500ft' section of the rule 5 (low flying) provisions, but not the other sections, in particular the requirement to be able to glide clear of the congested area in the event of an engine failure

D Terrain clearance and obeying the rule 5 provisions are the responsibility of ATC in this instance.

Questions and Answers
PAPER 5 *for the I M C Rating*

5 Without external visual references a pilot may interpret accelerating forwards as:

A A pitch up, whilst the air driven attitude indicator shows a pitch down

B A pitch up, whilst the air driven attitude indicator indicates a level attitude

C A pitch up, whilst the air driven attitude indicator also shows a pitch up

D A pitch down, whilst the air driven attitude indicator also shows a pitch down.

Complete the attached flight plan using an ICAO 1:500,000 Northern England chart

6 What is the Magnetic track from RETFORD to HARROGATE VRP?

A 327°

B 337°

C 330°

D 340°.

7 What is the most suitable Quadrantal Cruising Level between HARROGATE and DEAN CROSS assuming the QNH is 1003mb?

A FL65

B FL60

C FL45

D FL40.

8 What is the elapsed time for the leg from DEAN CROSS to TALLA?

A 20mins

B 27½mins

C 46½mins

D 39mins.

9 What is the Magnetic heading between TALLA and CUMBERNAULD?

A 314°

B 317°

C 328°

D 331°.

10 If you set course from RETFORD at 1132, what would be your ETA at CUMBERNAULD?

A 1325

B 1328

C 1331

D 1334.

11 The area identified as the Vale of York AIAA is:

A An area of intense aerial activity. A radar service is available from Linton 127.75 or Leeming 129.15

B An area of intense aerial activity. A radar service is available from Linton 129.15 or Leeming 127.75

C An area of itemised aerial activity. A radar service is available from Linton 129.15 or Leeming 127.75

D An area within which automatic information of aerial activity can be obtained by monitoring Linton 129.15 or Leeming 127.75.

---

12 What would be the minimum fuel uplift required (to the nearest lt) given:

Start, Taxy and Take-off and Climb	15lt
Retford to Cumbernauld @ 40lt/hr	
Approach and Missed Approach	20lt
Divert Cumbernauld to Edinburg @ 40lt/hr	
Approach and Landing	15lt
Holding 45mins @ 40lt/hr	
Reserve	40lt
Fuel in tank prior to refuel	45lt

A 165lt

B 159lt

C 175lt

D 120lt.

---

13 Using the answer in question 12 above, convert the fuel amount into US gallons. The correct answer is:

A 35 US gal

B 42 US gal

C 40 US gal

D 33 US gal.

---

14 Which statement below correctly describes the coverage of the glidepath element of a UK ILS?

A 8° either side of the localiser centreline up to 10nm from the runway threshold

B 10° either side of the localiser centreline up to 8nm from the runway threshold

C 35° either side of the localiser centreline up to 17nm from the runway threshold and 10° either side of the localiser centreline up to 25nm from the runway threshold

D 35° either side of the localiser centreline up to 10nm from the runway threshold and 10° either side of the localiser centreline up to 15nm from the runway threshold.

Questions and Answers
PAPER 5 *for the I M C Rating*

15 An aircraft is following a Magnetic track of 255° with a Magnetic heading of 265°. As you pass the 165° QDM to an NDB that is to the left of track the fixed card RBI will indicate a relative bearing of:

A 260°

B 270°

C 280°

D 290°.

16 In the event that the static source becomes blocked during a descent, which of the following correctly describes the effect on the ASI, VSI and Altimeter?

	ASI	VSI	Altimeter
A	Overread	Will change to zero ROC/ROD	Will overread
B	Read correctly	Will change to zero ROC/ROD	Will overread
C	Underread	Operate correctly	Will underread
D	Underread	Show erroneous ROC	Will underread

17 Upon tuning a VOR you hear the Morse Code TST. This indicates:

A The presence of a temporary side tone

B The VOR is radiating for test purposes and any bearing indications should be ignored

C The VOR is radiating for test purposes but any bearing indications may be relied upon

D The presence of a temporary transmitter.

18 An ILS indicator shows the Localiser needle to be 2 dots to the left of centre and the glidepath needle to be 2 dots below centre. This indicates that:

A The aircraft is to the left of centreline and below the glidepath

B The aircraft is to the right of centreline and above the glidepath

C The aircraft is to the right of centreline and below the glidepath

D The aircraft is to the left of centreline and above the glidepath.

19 A pilot flying an aircraft fitted with a typical civilian DME system notes that a TACAN paired frequency may be selected on the DME. In so doing, what useful navigational information will the pilot now receive from the TACAN?

A Slant range and bearing

B Horizontal range

C Slant range

D Horizontal range and bearing.

Questions and Answers for the IMC Rating PAPER 5

20 For an aircraft to be considered to be established on the final approach track of an instrument approach procedure it must be:

A   Exactly on track irrespective of type of approach aid being used

B   Exactly on track for the ILS and VOR, or within ± 5° of the required bearing for NDB (L)

C   Within half full scale deflection for the ILS and VOR, or within ± 5° of the required bearing for NDB (L)

D   Within half full scale deflection for the ILS and VOR, or within ± 10° of the required bearing for NDB (L).

21 The suction system is normally used to operate the ..... whilst the ...... is driven electrically. Select the response to complete the statement:

A   Turn co-ordinator; attitude indicator and heading indicator

B   Attitude indicator and heading indicator; turn co-ordinator

C   Attitude indicator and turn co-ordinator; heading indicator

D   Heading indicator and turn co-ordinator; attitude indicator.

22 Whilst receiving a Radar Information Service (RIS) you wish to change your cruising level. You should:

A   Only change your level when instructed by ATC

B   Inform ATC after you have changed level

C   Inform ATC before you change cruising level

D   Change level and inform ATC at next position report.

23 When an IFR flight is planned to enter Class E airspace, what ATC rules must be obeyed:

A   A flight plan (may be airborne), ATC clearance and radio communication are required and ATC instructions must be complied with

B   ATC clearance and radio communication are required and ATC instructions must be complied with

C   A flight plan (may be airborne), ATC clearance and radio communication are required and ATC instructions must be complied with and carriage of Mode C transponder is mandatory

D   ATC clearance and radio communication are required and ATC instructions must be complied with and carriage of Mode C transponder is mandatory.

24 The standard absolute minimum DH and MDH for an IMC-rated pilot flying a precision and non-precision approach respectively are:

A   OCH + 250ft   OCH + 200ft

B   OCH + 500ft   OCH + 600ft

C   500ft QFE   600ft QFE

D   550ft QFE   600ft QFE.

Questions and Answers
PAPER 5 *for the IMC Rating*

Refer to the instrument approach chart for runway 24 ILS at Edinburgh, then answer the question below:

25 You intend to fly the ILS for runway 24 to 'break cloud', then visually manoeuvre to land on runway 31.

What is the decision height for the ILS for an IMC-rated pilot, what is the minimum height for manoeuvring visually to the approach for runway 31, and what is the time from EDN to the missed approach point based on a groundspeed on approach of 100kts?

The system minimum is 250ft.

Visual Manoeuvring OCH 600ft QFE

	DH	Visual Manoeuvring Height	Time
A	410	600	1:40
B	600	600	1:24
C	500	650	1:40
D	500	600	1:40

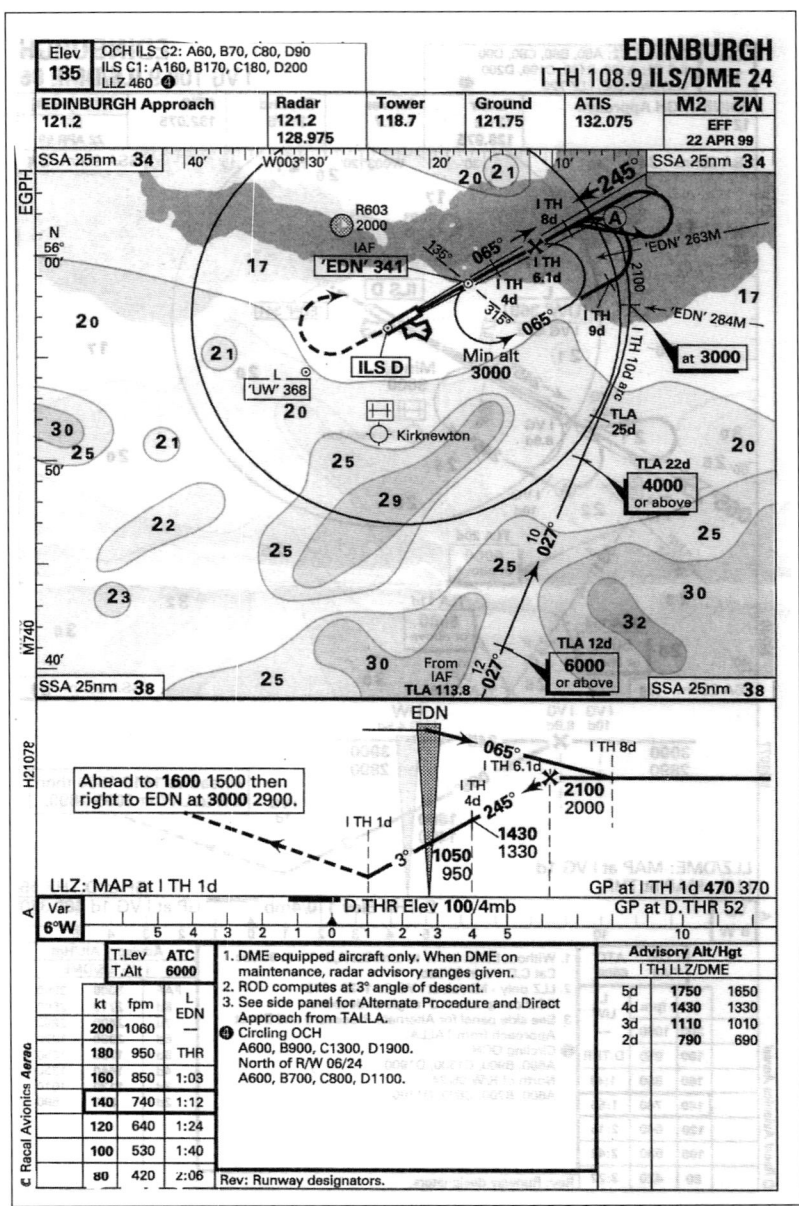

Questions and Answers for the IMC Rating PAPER 5

FLIGHT PLAN

Latitude and longitude are given as an aid to identification, but where locations and facilities are marked on the chart, their charted positions should be used.

From	To	Safety Alt ft amsl	FL/Alt	TAS kt	Trk T	W/V	Hdg T	Varn	Hdg M	GS kt	Dist nm	Time min	ETA
RETFORD (531650N 0005705W)	VRP HARROGATE (535930W 0013136W)	1900	FL45	120		290/10		5°W					
VRP HARROGATE	DEAN CROSS (DCS) (544319N W0032026W)	4500		120		300/10		6°W					
DCS	TALLA (TLA) (553010N 0032550W)	4100	FL50	120		330/20		6°W					
TLA	CUMBERNAULD (555830N 0035828W)	4100	FL45	120		330/20		7°W					
ALTERNATE										Totals			
CUMBERNAULD	EDINBURGH (555709N 0032146W)	2100	Descent as required	120		300/15		7°W					

Note: Safety Altitude is derived from the higher of:

(i) the highest ground plus 1299 feet; or

(ii) the highest structure plus 1000 feet; rounded up to the next 100 feet, within 5nm of track.

5.9

Questions and Answers
PAPER 5 *for the IMC Rating*

Reference Section
ANSWER PAPER 5

FLIGHT PLAN

Latitude and longitude are given as an aid to identification, but where locations and facilities are marked on the chart, their charted positions should be used.

From	To	Safety Alt ft amsl	FL/Alt	TAS kt	Trk T	W/V	Hdg T	Varn	Hdg M	GS kt	Dist nm	Time min	ETA
RETFORD (531650N 0005705W)	VRP HARROGATE (535930N 0013136W)	1900	FL45	120	335	290/10	332	5°W	337	112	47	25	
VRP HARROGATE	DEAN CROSS (DCS) (544319N 0032026W)	4500	FL65	120	305	300/10	305	6°W	311	110	77	42	
DCS	TALLA (TLA) (553010N 0032550W)	4100	FL50	120	359	330/20	354	6°W	360	102	46·5	27·5	
TLA	CUMBERNAULD (555830N 0035828W)	4100	FL45	120	323	330/20	324	7°W	331	100	35·5	21·5	
									Totals		206	116	
ALTERNATE													
CUMBERNAULD	EDINBURGH (555709N 0032146W)	2100	Descent as required	120	094	300/15	091	7°W	098	133	20·5	9	

Note: Safety Altitude is derived from the higher of:

(i) the highest ground plus 1299 feet; or

(ii) the highest structure plus 1000 feet;

rounded up to the next 100 feet, within 5nm of track.

Instrument Meteorlogical Conditions

ANSWER PAPER 5

1 D

Note, the quadrantal rule applies to flights outside controlled airspace only.

Further reference: The Private Pilot's Licence Course Book 2 (Air Law and Radiotelephony), VFR / IFR and Aeronautical Information Service sections; The Private Pilot's Licence Course Book 3 (Navigation, Meteorology and Flight Planning), The Full Flight Plan section.

2 A

CAP 53, Part 2 refers.

3 A

Further reference: The Private Pilot's Licence Course Book 2 (Air Law and Radiotelephony), Airspace Restrictions section.

4 C

Note that the aircraft has been offered a SVFR clearance.
Further reference: The Private Pilot's Licence Course Book 2 (Air Law and Radiotelephony), Rules of the Air and VFR / IFR sections.

5 C

The only force the pilot experiences in level flight at constant speed in his own weight. If the aircraft accelerates forward an inertial force is produced by the acceleration that acts as shown. The resultant of these forces in an accelerating aircraft operates similarly to the weight force in a climbing aircraft. Because the otoliths act much like a spirit level the pilot may mistake acceleration for a pitch up.

Accelerating aircraft   **Climbing aircraft**

inertial force

weight   resultant   weight

The inertial force generated by acceleration affects the pendulous unit used to keep the attitude indicator gyro spin axis vertical. This will be seen by the pilot as a small transient error in pitch and roll. In particular acceleration will cause the attitude indicator to indicate a momentary pitch up.

6 D

From the completed flight plan track (T) is 335°, westerly variation is added, thus
335° + 5°W = track 340° (M)

Further reference: The Private Pilot's Licence Course Book 3 (Navigation, Meteorology and Flight Planning), Aeronautical Maps section.

ANSWER PAPER 5

7 A

From the completed flight plan, track (T) 305° + variation 6°W = track (M) 311°.

This puts the aircraft in the EVEN + 500 ft sector when determining quadrantal cruising level.

The safety altitude between Harrogate and Dean Cross is 4500ft.

Now check the difference between QNH and standard pressure:
QNH   1003mb
Standard Pressure   1013mb
Difference   10mb; @ 30ft/mb = 300ft.

QNH is low, so add 300ft to safe altitude. This confirms that FL45 is not available, as the aircraft will have to descend to 4200ft QNH to cruise at FL45 which is below the safe altitude. The next quadrantal level in this case is FL65.

Further reference: The Private Pilot's Licence Course Book 3 (Navigation, Meteorology and Flight Planning), Vertical Navigation section.

8 B

Taken from the completed flight plan. As a gross error check, note that there is a headwind on this leg, so groundspeed is less than airspeed. The answer should be 27·5 minutes.

Further reference: The Private Pilot's Licence Course Book 3 (Navigation, Meteorology and Flight Planning), Navigation Principles 1 section.

9 D

Taken from the completed flight plan.

Further reference: The Private Pilot's Licence Course Book 3 (Navigation, Meteorology and Flight Planning), Navigation Principles 1 section.

10 B

From the completed flight plan, the total en-route time is 116 minutes.

Set course   11.32
En route time   1.56 (i.e. 116 minutes)
ETA   =   13.28

11 B

This information can be found in the UK AIP ENR 5.2 Section and also on the ICAO 1:500,000 Northern England chart.

Further reference: The Private Pilot's Licence Course Book 2 (Air Law and Radiotelephony), Airspace Restrictions section.

Instrument Meteorological Conditions

ANSWER PAPER 5

12 B

Using the flight computer, calculate fuel required as below:

Retford to Cumbernauld 116 minutes @ 40lt/hr = 78lt
Cumbernauld to Edinburgh 9 minutes @ 40lt/hr = 6lt
Hold - 45 minutes @ 40lt/hr = 30lt

Complete the table by adding all quantities 15 + **78** + 20 + 6 + 15 + **30** + 40 = 204lt

Now deduct fuel already in the tank: 204lt
                                               - 45lt

fuel uplift required   159lt

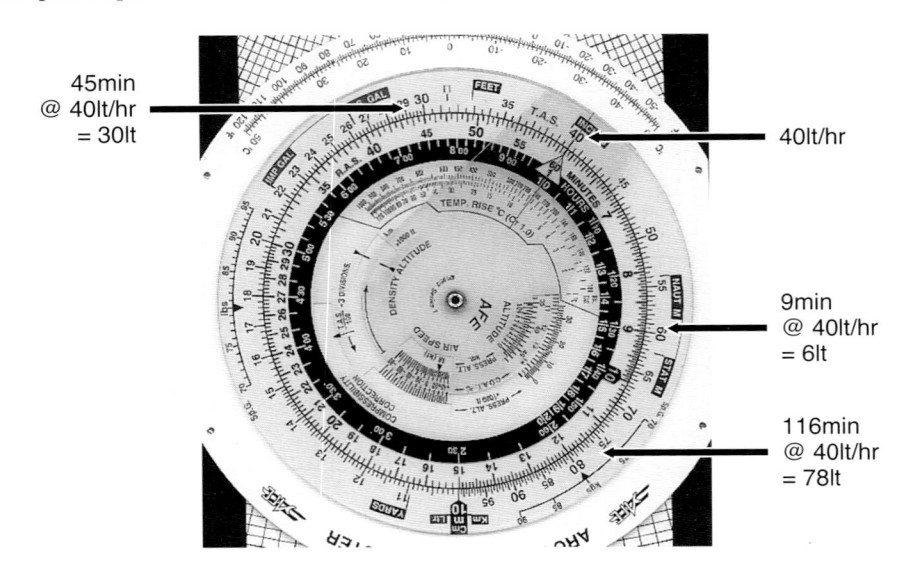

Further reference: The Private Pilot's Licence Course Book 3 (Navigation, Meteorology and Flight Planning), Fuel Planning section.

13 B

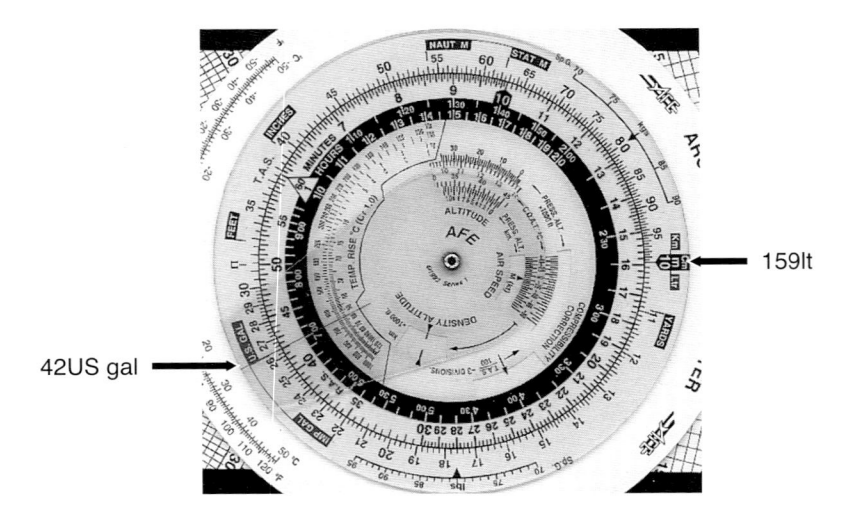

Further reference: The Private Pilot's Licence Course Book 3 (Navigation, Meteorology and Flight Planning), Fuel Planning section.

14 A

There is usually a pink AIC current that describes the ILS.

Reference Section

ANSWER PAPER 5

15 A

Magnetic track   255°

HI Heading   265°

RBI indication   =   HDG - QDM
                     265 - 165 = 100°

NDB is left of track so the Relative Bearing will be 360° - 100° = 260°

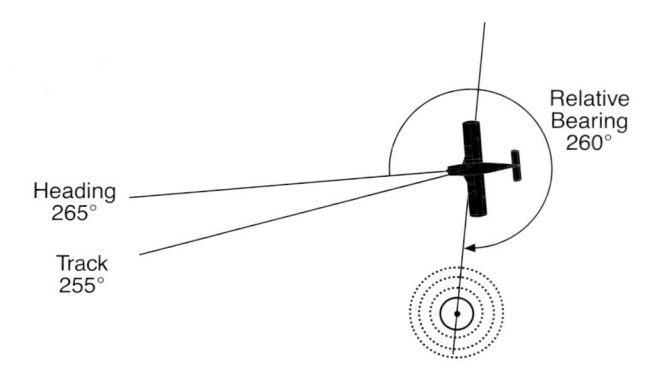

16 A

The lower static pressure in the ASI case will allow the ASI needle to show a higher than actual airspeed - overreading.

The VSI will fall to zero rate of climb / rate of descent because no static air is entering the instrument. The Altimeter will continue to read the altitude at which the blockage occurred, therefore in the descent it will be overreading (it is showing an altitude greater than actual).

17 B

UK AIP GEN 3 refers.

18 B

Remember the needles are command indicators. Fly towards them to correct the situation. In this case the aircraft is right of centreline and above the glidepath.

19 C

TACAN is a military radio navigation aid, giving both range and bearing information. An aircraft equipped with a typical civilian DME may interrogate a TACAN, but only range, groundspeed and time will be displayed. The airborne DME equipment is not able to utilise the bearing element of the TACAN system. Answer C is correct because the DME displays slant range.

20 C

UK AIP ENR 1.5 refers.

21 B

Generally a suction system powers the attitude indicator and direction indicator whilst the turn co-ordinator is electrically powered. This will allow the pilot to continue instrument flight to a safe conclusion should one or other of the systems fail.

22 C

UK AIP ENR 1.6 refers.

Further reference: The Private Pilot's Licence Course Book 2 (Air Law and Radiotelephony), En-Route Procedures section.

Instrument Meteorlogical Conditions

ANSWER PAPER 5

23 A

UK AIP ENR 1.3 refers.

Further reference: The Private Pilot's Licence Course Book 2 (Air Law and Radiotelephony), Aeronautical Information Service section; The Private Pilot's Licence Course Book 3 (Navigation, Meteorology and Flight Planning), The Full Flight Plan section.

24 C

UK AIP AD 1.1.2 section refers.

25 D

The OCH (taken from the top of the chart) is 160ft.

OCH	160ft
+ PEC	50ft
+ IMC allowance	200ft
=	410ft

However, the absolute minimum DH for an IMC-rated pilot flying a precision approach is 500ft, as this is higher, 500ft becomes the Decision Height.

Visual Manoeuvring is based purely on the Visual Manoeuvring OCH for a category A, no allowances need to be added, therefore 600ft is the correct answer.

Using the groundspeed/time table on the chart the time at 100kt is 1 minute 40 seconds.

Questions and Answers
for the IMC Rating **PAPER 6**

Instructions

1 Time allowed 2 hours.

2 Twenty five multi-choice questions each carrying 4 marks. Marks are not deducted for wrong answers. The pass mark is 72% (i.e. 18 questions or more must be answered correctly).

3 Unless otherwise specified, the questions relate to a UK licenced pilot, operating a UK registered aircraft in UK airspace.

4 Read each question carefully as there is only one answer which is correct.

5 Remember examination technique, you are advised to pass over questions that seem difficult at first sight and return to them when you have answered the others.

Questions and Answers for the IMC Rating — PAPER 6

1 The holder of an IMC rating who wishes to fly in Class D airspace:

A May only do so in VMC

B Must comply with the Specified Minimum Weather Conditions

C May accept a Special VFR clearance if the visibility is less than 3km

D May accept an IFR clearance provided a full flight plan has been filed.

2 The IMC rating is valid for a period of:

A 13 months from date of test

B 25 months from date of issue

C 25 months from date of test

D 13 months from date of issue.

3 You are flying IFR at FL95 outside controlled airspace and wish to descend. The highest obstacle within 5nm of your track is 2750ft amsl. Given the Regional QNH is 965mb (assume 1mb = 30ft), your track is 183°(T) (variation 5°E) the lowest Quadrantal Flight Level you may descend to is:

A FL65

B FL55

C FL45

D FL35.

4 "CAVOK" is forecast in a TAF. To what level could the cloud ceiling fall before a new TAF must be issued?

A 4900ft

B 2500ft

C 1000ft

D 1600ft.

5 Whilst accelerating in level flight the pilot is subject to the force of gravity and the inertial force of acceleration. The otoliths may interpret the resultant of these forces as a?

A Pitch up

B Pitch down

C Yaw left

D Yaw right.

Questions and Answers
PAPER 6 *for the I M C Rating*

Complete the attached flight plan using an ICAO 1:500,000 Southern England chart

6 What is the Magnetic track between LAMBOURNE and BOVINGDON?

A 281°

B 285°

C 277°

D 275°.

7 What is the Magnetic heading between BOVINGDON and DROITWICH?

A 285°

B 304°

C 313°

D 295°.

8 What is the groundspeed for the leg between DROITWICH and HALFPENNY GREEN?

A 100 kt

B 120 kt

C 131 kt

D 140 kt.

9 What is the flight time between Hawarden and the alternate?

A 18 mins

B 12 mins

C 15·5 mins

D 21·5 mins

10 What would be the lowest Quadrantal cruising level between BOVINGDON and DROITWICH (assume QNH is 1014mb)?

A FL30

B FL35

C FL40

D FL45.

11 You set course overhead SOUTHEND at 1312 UTC. Based on flight plan time what is your ETA at HAWARDEN (rounded down to the nearest minute)?

A 1443

B 1458

C 1452

D 1432.

12 Given a fuel consumption of 8US gal/hr how much fuel, (to the nearest litre) would be required to complete the flight:

Start, Taxy and Take-off and Climb	2US gal
Southend to Hawarden @ 8US gal/hr	
Approach and Missed Approach	2US gal
Hawarden to Shawbury @ 8US gal/hr	
Approach and Landing	1US gal
Holding 45mins @ 8US gal/hr	
Reserve	8US gal

A 111lt

B 120lt

C 125lt

D 107lt.

13 Given:
Aircraft Maximum T/O Weight 2500lb.
Aircraft Maximum Landing Weight 2400lb.
You take-off at maximum weight but discover that your suction system has failed and you elect to abandon your flight and land. The fuel consumption is 8imp gal/hr with SG of .72. Ignoring allowances for taxy and take-off how long must you remain airborne before the aircraft weight will allow you to return and land:

A 91 minutes

B 104 minutes

C 139 minutes

D 165 minutes.

14 You are receiving a Radar Advisory Service (RAS) from Thames Radar. Due to a traffic avoidance manoeuvre you are positioned 3nm south of Potters Bar at 2000ft QNH when Thames Radar offer you a direct route to BOVINGDON VOR. Who is responsible for obtaining clearance through the Elstree Aerodrome Traffic Zone:

A Thames Radar

B The pilot

C London FIS

D Thames Radar if the aircraft is equipped with a Mode C transponder.

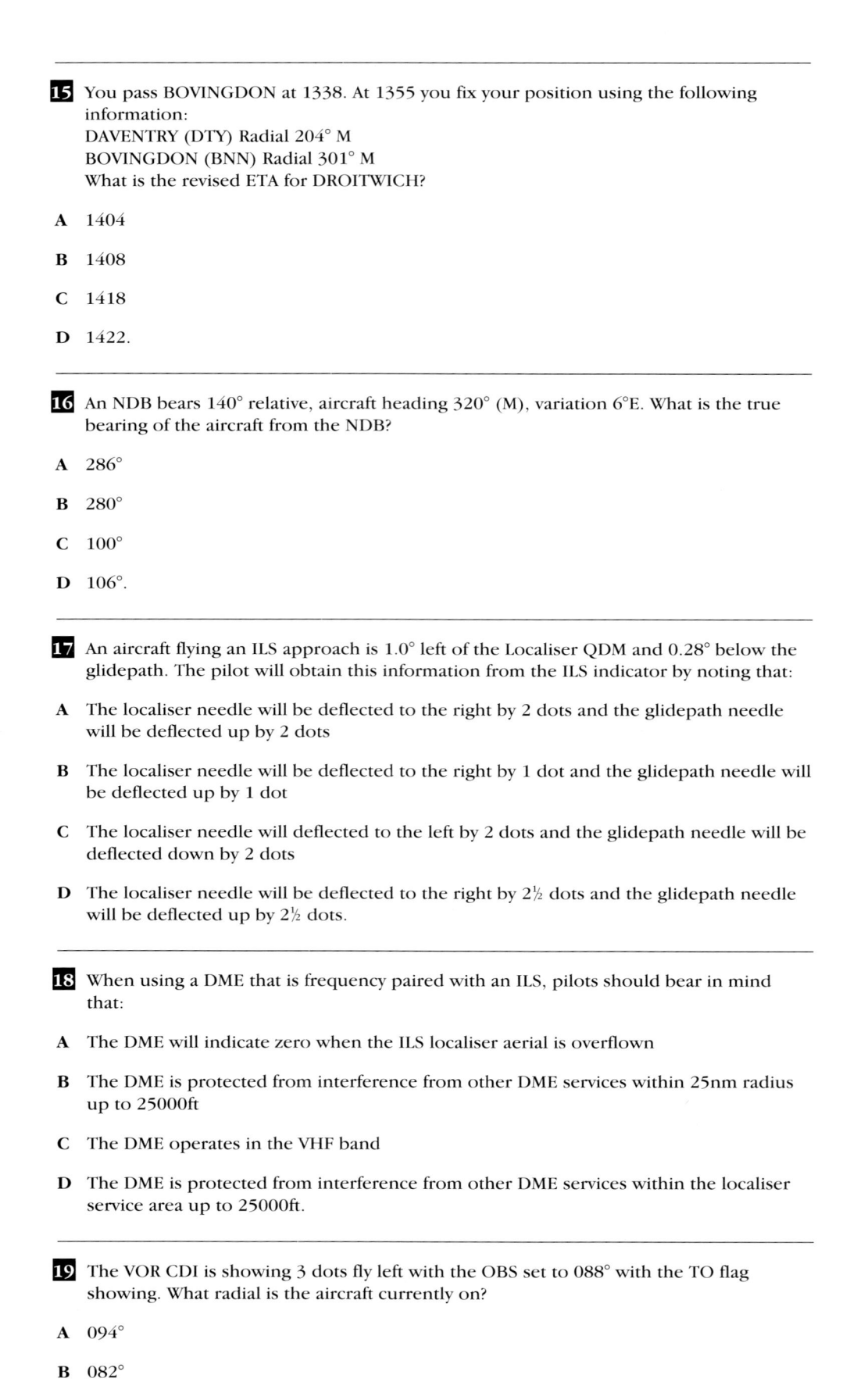

Questions and Answers
PAPER 6 *for the IMC Rating*

15 You pass BOVINGDON at 1338. At 1355 you fix your position using the following information:
DAVENTRY (DTY) Radial 204° M
BOVINGDON (BNN) Radial 301° M
What is the revised ETA for DROITWICH?

A 1404

B 1408

C 1418

D 1422.

16 An NDB bears 140° relative, aircraft heading 320° (M), variation 6°E. What is the true bearing of the aircraft from the NDB?

A 286°

B 280°

C 100°

D 106°.

17 An aircraft flying an ILS approach is 1.0° left of the Localiser QDM and 0.28° below the glidepath. The pilot will obtain this information from the ILS indicator by noting that:

A The localiser needle will be deflected to the right by 2 dots and the glidepath needle will be deflected up by 2 dots

B The localiser needle will be deflected to the right by 1 dot and the glidepath needle will be deflected up by 1 dot

C The localiser needle will deflected to the left by 2 dots and the glidepath needle will be deflected down by 2 dots

D The localiser needle will be deflected to the right by 2½ dots and the glidepath needle will be deflected up by 2½ dots.

18 When using a DME that is frequency paired with an ILS, pilots should bear in mind that:

A The DME will indicate zero when the ILS localiser aerial is overflown

B The DME is protected from interference from other DME services within 25nm radius up to 25000ft

C The DME operates in the VHF band

D The DME is protected from interference from other DME services within the localiser service area up to 25000ft.

19 The VOR CDI is showing 3 dots fly left with the OBS set to 088° with the TO flag showing. What radial is the aircraft currently on?

A 094°

B 082°

C 274°

D 262°.

Questions and Answers
for the IMC Rating PAPER 6

20 For an IMC-rated pilot, what are the absolute minimum Decision Height, Minimum Circling Height (for a category A aircraft) and RVR figures permissible for making an instrument approach?

	Decision Height	Minimum Circling Height	RVR
A	500ft	500ft	1800m
B	600ft	400ft	2000m
C	500ft	650ft	1900m
D	500ft	400ft	1800m.

21 When flying a typical single engine single pilot training aircraft, you suspect failure of the attitude indicator and heading indicator. To verify a system failure which of the following would you check:

A The suction gauge

B The ammeter

C The oil pressure gauge

D The alternate static source.

22 To assist an Approach Control Unit at an airfield outside controlled airspace to provide a better service, pilots flying IFR are strongly recommended to:

A Fly directly overhead the airfield to ensure separation from instrument approach procedures

B Make contact when at least 5 minutes flying time or 15nm from the Aerodrome Traffic Zone boundary, whichever is greater

C Avoid flying IFR within 10nm radius at less than 3000ft above an aerodrome having Approach Control

D Avoid flying IFR within 20nm radius at less than 3000ft above an aerodrome having Approach Control.

Refer to this extract from the UK AIP

EGBO AD 2.19 – RADIO NAVIGATION AND LANDING AIDS							
Type Category (Variation)	IDENT	Frequency	Hours of Operation ##		Antenna site co-ordinates	Elevation of DME transmitting antenna	Remarks
			Winter	Summer			
			# and by arrangement				
1	2	3	4		5	6	7
NDB	HG	356.0 kHz	H24	H24	*523103N 0021541W		On AD. Range 10 nm.

23 At what range from HALFPENNY GREEN would you begin to receive reliable bearing information from the HG NDB?

A 10nm

B 15nm

C 20nm

D 24nm.

Questions and Answers
PAPER 6 *for the IMC Rating*

24 As an IMC-rated pilot you plan to make an ILS approach to airfield 'A' which is outside controlled airspace, followed by a VFR transit to land at airfield 'B', also outside controlled airspace. Airfield 'B' does not have an Instrument Approach Procedure (IAP). Given that the ILS approach has a minimum RVR of 650m, what are:

- the minimum RVR for the ILS at airfield 'A'

- the minimum visibility for the VFR transit to airfield 'B'

- the minimum RVR/visibility for landing at airfield 'B'?

Assume that the visual transit will be carried-out at less than 140kts IAS and below 3000ft amsl.

	ILS	VFR Transit to airfield 'B'	Landing at airfield 'B'
A	650m	1900m	1500m
B	1800m	2000m	1500m
C	1800m	1500m	1800m
D	650m	1800m	1500m.

25 Given the following data:
OCH for NDB/DME Runway 04 - 380ft aircraft Category A
Visual Manoeuvring (Circling) OCH - 500ft aircraft Category A
System minima 300ft
You intend to fly the NDB/DME Approach to Runway 04, then circle to land on runway 09. The Minimum Descent Height (MDH) and Visual Manoeuvring (Circling) OCH you should use are:

A 580ft; 500ft

B 600ft; 500ft

C 600ft; 400ft

D 630ft; 500ft.

Reference Section
ANSWER PAPER 6

FLIGHT PLAN

Latitude and longitude are given as an aid to identification, but where locations and facilities are marked on the chart, their charted positions should be used.

From	To	Safety Alt ft amsl	FL/Alt	TAS kt	Trk T	W/V	Hdg T	Varn	Hdg M	GS kt	Dist nm	Time min	ETA
SOUTHEND (513417N 0004144E)	LAMBOURNE (LAM) (513846N 0000906E)	1800	2400	100		190/20		4°W					
LAM	BOVINGDON (BNN) (514334N 0003259W)	2000	2400	115		190/20		4°W					
BNN	DROITWICH (521700N 0021000W)	2200		115		190/20		5°W					
DROITWICH	HALFPENNY GREEN (HG) (523103N 0021535W)	2400	FL45	115		205/20		5°W					
HG	HAWARDEN (531041N 0025840W)	2700	Descent as required	115		205/20		6°W					
ALTERNATE										Totals			
HAWARDEN	SHAWBURY (524753N 0024004W)	2000	2500	115		205/20		6°W					

Note: Safety Altitude is derived from the higher of:

(i) the highest ground plus 1299 feet; or

(ii) the highest structure plus 1000 feet; rounded up to the next 100 feet, within 5nm of track.

Instrument Meteorlogical Conditions
ANSWERS PAPER 6 *for the I M C Rating*

Reference Section
ANSWER PAPER 6

FLIGHT PLAN

Latitude and longitude are given as an aid to identification, but where locations and facilities are marked on the chart, their charted positions should be used.

From	To	Safety Alt ft amsl	FL/Alt	TAS kt	Trk T	W/V	Hdg T	Varn	Hdg M	GS kt	Dist nm	Time min	ETA
SOUTHEND (513417N 0004144E)	LAMBOURNE (LAM) (513846N 0000906E)	1800	2400	100	283	190/20	271	4°W	275	99	21	12·5	
LAM	BOVINGDON (BNN) (514334N 0003259W)	2000	2400	115	281	190/20	271	4°W	275	114	26·5	14	
BNN	DROITWICH (521700N 0021000W)	2200	FL45	115	299	190/20	290	5°W	295	120	68·5	34	
DROITWICH	HALFPENNY GREEN (HG) (523103N 0021535W)	2400	FL45	115	346	205/20	340	5°W	345	130	15	7	
HG	HAWARDEN (531041N 0025840W)	2700	Descent as required	115	327	205/20	319	6°W	325	124	47·5	23	
									Totals		178	90·5	
ALTERNATE													
HAWARDEN	SHAWBURY (524753N 0024004W)	2000	2500	115	156	205/20	163	6°W	169	101	26	15·5	

Note: Safety Altitude is derived from the higher of:

(i) the highest ground plus 1299 feet; or

(ii) the highest structure plus 1000 feet; rounded up to the next 100 feet, within 5nm of track.

6.11

Instrument Meteorlogical Conditions
ANSWERS PAPER 6 *for the IMC Rating*

1 D

Further reference: CAP 53 Part 2; The Private Pilot's Licence Course Book 3 (Navigation, Meteorology and Flight Planning), The Full Flight Plan section.

2 C

CAP 53 Part 2 refers.

3 B

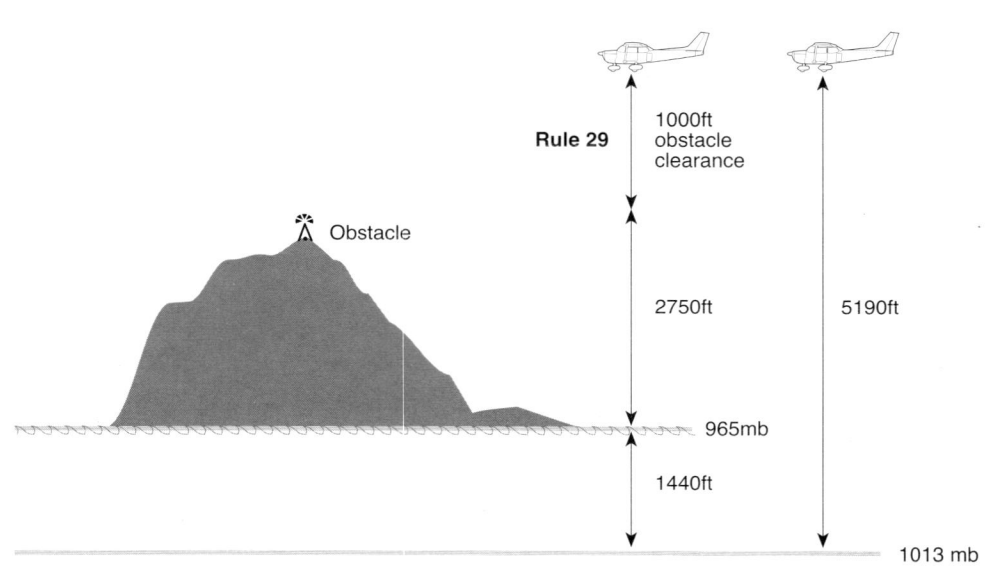

Difference between QNH and Standard Pressure is 48mb. This equates (at 1mb/30 ft) to 1440ft. As QNH is low, altimeter will read high when set to 1013mb.

Obstacle + 1000ft equates to 5190ft with altimeter set to 1013mb.

Next determine the track (M). Track (T) 183°, + variation 5°E (remember, 'East is Least') = track (M) 178°
Thus a Flight Level of ODD + 500ft is required.

The lowest Flight Level useable is FL55. FL35 would compromise the IFR obstacle clearance requirements.

Further reference: The Private Pilot's Licence Course Book 3 (Navigation, Meteorology and Flight Planning), Vertical Navigation section; The Private Pilot's Licence Course Book 2 (Air Law and Radiotelephony), VFR / IFR section.

4 D

Further reference: The Private Pilot's Licence Course Book 3 (Navigation, Meteorology and Flight Planning), Aviation Weather Reports and Forecasts section.

5 A

The only force the pilot experiences in level flight at constant speed is his own weight. If the aircraft accelerates forward an additional force is produced by the acceleration which acts as shown. The resultant of these forces in an accelerating aircraft operates similarly to the weight force in a climbing aircraft. Because the otoliths act like a spirit level, the pilot may mistake acceleration for a pitch up.

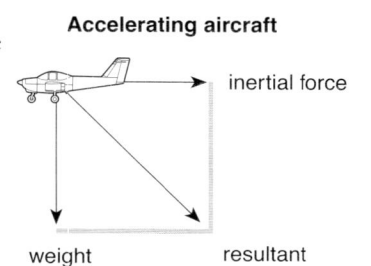

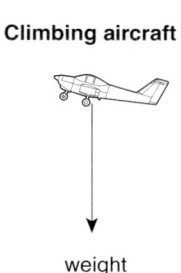

Reference Section

ANSWER PAPER 6

6 B

From the completed flight plan track (T) is 281° (T). The Magnetic variation for the area is 4°W, 'West is Best' so add: 281 + 4 = 285° (M).

Further reference: The Private Pilot's Licence Course Book 3 (Navigation, Meteorology and Flight Planning), Aeronautical Maps section.

7 D

Taken from the completed flight plan.

Further reference: The Private Pilot's Licence Course Book 3 (Navigation, Meteorology and Flight Planning), Navigation Principles 1 section.

8 C

As a 'gross error' check note that angle between wind and track gives a tailwind.

Further reference: The Private Pilot's Licence Course Book 3 (Navigation, Meteorology and Flight Planning), Navigation Principles 1 section.

9 C

Taken from the flight plan.

Further reference: The Private Pilot's Licence Course Book 3 (Navigation, Meteorology and Flight Planning), Navigation Principles 1 and Navigation Principles 2 sections.

10 D

From the completed flight plan the safety altitude on this leg is 2200ft. This is found on the 1:500,000 chart by taking the spot height of 876ft amsl south of Halton. Add to this the allowance for unmarked obstructions of 299ft and the IFR obstacle allowance of 1000ft (2175ft). Now round up to the next hundred. This gives 2200ft.

Compare this figure with the highest obstacle (masts 900ft amsl north east of Droitwich), plus IFR allowance; 900ft + 1000ft = 1900ft.

The MSA is the higher of the two figures - 2200ft.

The magnetic track can be taken from the flight plan (299° + 5°W) = 304° (M). This puts the leg in the quadrant for even FLs + 500ft.

As QNH is more than Standard Pressure (1013mb), the lowest correct quadrantal Flight Level above the MSA can be used without compromising, this will be FL45

Further reference: The Private Pilot's Licence Course Book 3 (Navigation, Meteorology and Flight Planning), Vertical Navigation section; The Private Pilot's Licence Course Book 2 (Air Law and Radiotelephony), VFR / IFR section.

11 A

From the completed flight plan add up the leg times. The total should be 1 hour 30·5 minutes.
Add this to the set course time of 1312 to give an ETA of 1443 (rounded down to the nearest minute).

Instrument Meteorological Conditions

ANSWERS PAPER 6 *for the IMC Rating*

12 C

Using the flight computer set at 8US gal/hr calculate:

Southend to Hawarden	90 minutes @ 8US gal/hr =	12US gal
Hawarden to Shawbury	15·5 minutes @ 8US gal/hr =	2US gal
Hold	45 minutes @ 8US gal/hr =	6US gal

Complete the table by adding all quantities 2 + 12 + 2 + 2 + 1 + 6 + 8 = 33US gal.
33US gal = 125lt.

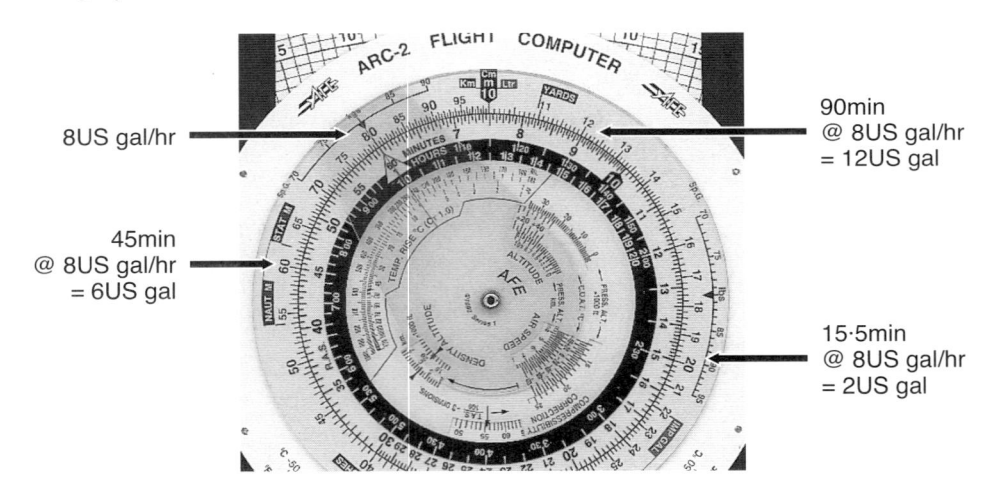

- 8US gal/hr
- 90min @ 8US gal/hr = 12US gal
- 45min @ 8US gal/hr = 6US gal
- 15·5min @ 8US gal/hr = 2US gal

Further reference: The Private Pilot's Licence Course Book 3 (Navigation, Meteorology and Flight Planning), Fuel Planning section.

13 B

100lb of fuel must be burnt before the aircraft can land

100lb @ SG ·72 = 13·8imp gal

13·8imp gal @ 8imp gal/hr = 104min

Further reference: The Private Pilot's Licence Course Book 3 (Navigation, Meteorology and Flight Planning), Performance section.

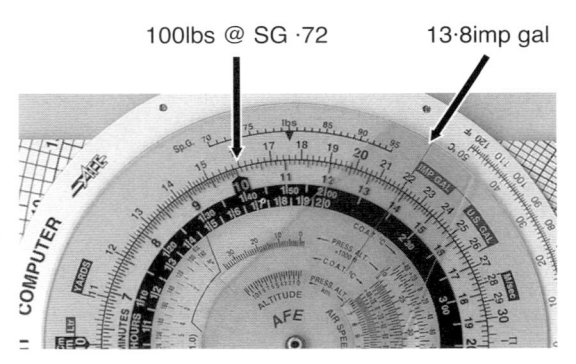

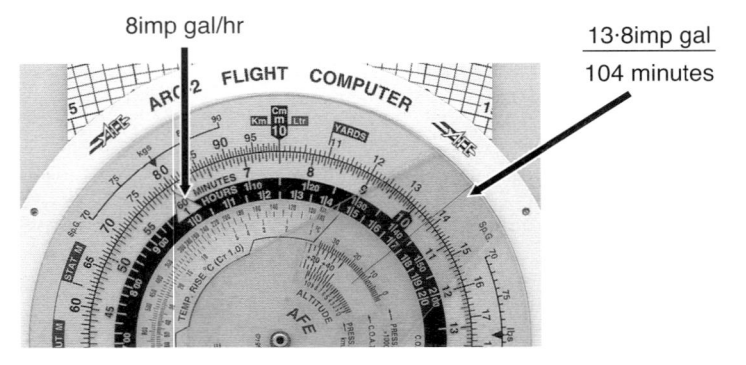

- 100lbs @ SG ·72
- 13·8imp gal
- 8imp gal/hr
- 13·8imp gal / 104 minutes

14 B

UK AIP ENR 1.6 refers.

Further reference: The Private Pilot's Licence Course Book 2 (Air Law and Radiotelephony), En Route Procedures and Rules of the Air and ATC section.

Reference Section
ANSWER PAPER 6

15 C

Plot the radials on a 1:500,000 chart, this fix shows the position as Upper Heyford disused airfield. Thus 29nm have been flown in 17 minutes.
Use the flight computer to calculate the groundspeed of 102kt.

Based on this speed it will take 23 minutes to complete the leg.

So revised ETA for DROITWICH is 1355 (the time of the fix overhead Upper Heyford) + 23 minutes = 1418.

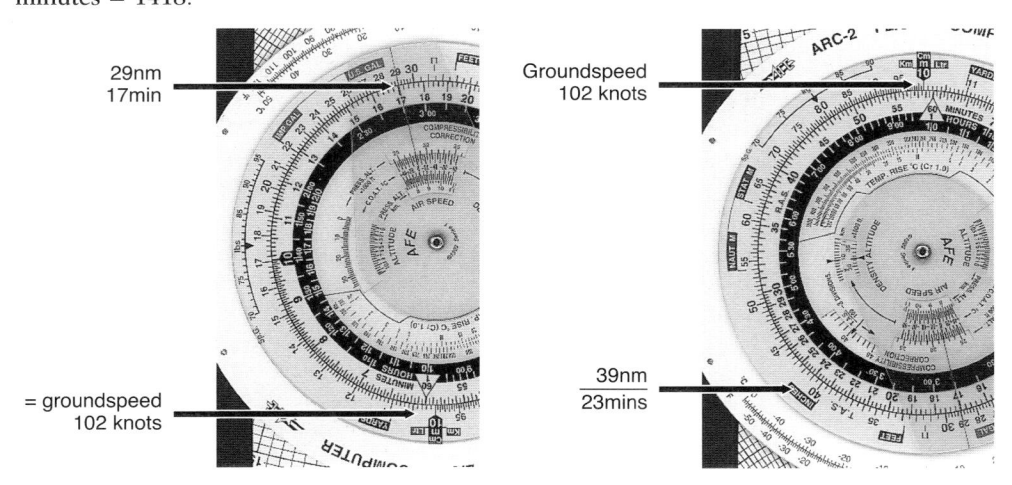

Further reference: The Private Pilot's Licence Course Book 3 (Navigation, Meteorology and Flight Planning), Navigation Principles 2 section.

16 A

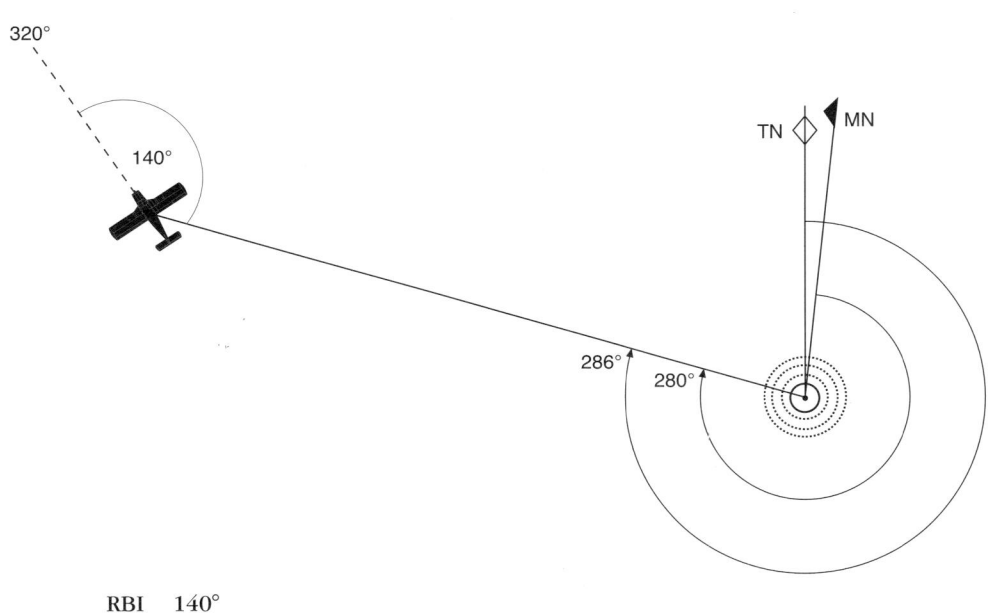

```
         RBI    140°
+ Heading       320°
       =        460°
       -        360°
       =        100°
```

Thus the QDM (to the NDB) is 100° (M).

By removing variation (6°E), the true bearing to the NDB is found, 106° (T)

Add 180° to obtain the bearing **from**:

106 + 180 = 286° (T)

Instrument Meteorlogical Conditions
ANSWERS PAPER 6 *for the I M C Rating*

17 A

For every 0·5° the aircraft deviates from the ILS QDM, the localiser CDI will be deflected by 1 dot. Remember that the needle will indicate the direction to fly in order to return to the ILS QDM, 2 dots = 1° and with the aircraft to the left of the ILS QDM the CDI needle will be deflected to the right.

For every 0·14° the aircraft deviates from the ILS glideslope the glidepath needle will be deflected by 1 dot. Remember that the needle will indicate the direction to fly in order to regain the ILS glidepath, 2 dots = 0·28° and with the aircraft below the ILS glidepath the needle will be deflected up.

There is usually a current pink AIC re. the ILS.

18 D

There is usually a current pink AIC re. the ILS.

19 D

The VOR indicator is set in relation to a **track** of 088° (M), which means that the aircraft is attempting to follow the 268° radial. Interpretation of the indicator reveals the aircraft to be right of track by 6°. Thus the Track Made Good is 088° - 6° = 082°. This means the aircraft is currently on the 262° radial.

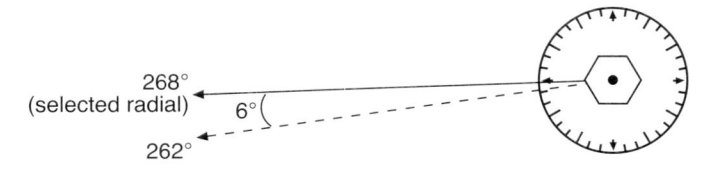

20 D

UK AIP AD 1.1.2 and ENR 1.5.

21 A

The attitude indicator and the heading indicator are typically powered by the suction system

Further reference: The Private Pilot's Licence Course Book 4 (Technical) The Aircraft Instruments.

22 C

UK AIP GEN 3.3 refers.

23 A

Refer to the range quoted in the extract from the UK AIP.

24 C

UK AIP AD 1.1.2 and ENR 1.5 refers.

Further reference: The Private Pilot's Licence Course Book 2 (Air Law and Radiotelephony), VFR/IFR section.

25 B

System minima   300ft
OCH Cat A   380ft.

Thus OCH is higher so add IMC allowance to this figure.

MDH:
380 + 200 = 580ft, this is rounded up to **600ft** as this is recommended minimum for a non-precision approach by an IMC-rated pilot.

Visual Manoeuvring (Circling) OCH remains 500ft, no allowance needs to be added. So minima for this approach are:

MDH   600ft
VM(C)   500ft.

UK AIP AD 1.1.2 and ENR 1.5 refers.

Reference Section

ANSWERS PAPERS 1-6

PAPER 1	1 A	6 C	11 A	16 A	21 C
	2 D	7 B	12 D	17 D	22 B
	3 B	8 B	13 A	18 C	23 D
	4 C	9 C	14 C	19 A	24 B
	5 D	10 C	15 C	20 B	25 C

PAPER 2	1 D	6 C	11 B	16 C	21 C
	2 C	7 C	12 A	17 B	22 D
	3 B	8 B	13 B	18 A	23 A
	4 C	9 D	14 A	19 C	24 C
	5 A	10 A	15 C	20 C	25 C

PAPER 3	1 B	6 A	11 C	16 D	21 A
	2 B	7 B	12 C	17 A	22 A
	3 B	8 D	13 C	18 D	23 B
	4 C	9 B	14 D	19 D	24 C
	5 C	10 C	15 C	20 D	25 B

PAPER 4	1 C	6 A	11 A	16 B	21 A
	2 A	7 C	12 B	17 D	22 B
	3 A	8 B	13 A	18 C	23 C
	4 C	9 D	14 D	19 C	24 D
	5 B	10 C	15 B	20 A	25 C

PAPER 5	1 D	6 D	11 B	16 A	21 B
	2 A	7 A	12 B	17 B	22 C
	3 A	8 B	13 B	18 B	23 A
	4 C	9 D	14 A	19 C	24 C
	5 C	10 B	15 A	20 C	25 D

PAPER 6	1 D	6 B	11 A	16 A	21 A
	2 C	7 D	12 C	17 A	22 C
	3 B	8 C	13 B	18 D	23 A
	4 D	9 C	14 B	19 D	24 C
	5 A	10 D	15 C	20 D	25 B